The Complete Front-End Interview Guide

Angular, Node.js, React, Next.js, Vue.js & TypeScript

Master The Fundamentals And Advanced Concepts, Become A Front-End Expert With Comprehensive Interview Preparation

Nirbhay Chauhan

About the Author

Nirbhay Chauhan: The Complete Front-End Interview Guide: Angular, Node.js, React, Next.js, Vue.js, & TypeScript

Nirbhay Chauhan is a passionate software developer with a deep understanding of the .NET landscape. His journey began in 2000, diving headfirst into the world of computers with DOS and programming languages like C and FoxPro. This early exposure ignited a lifelong love of technology and problem-solving.

Nirbhay's career took a pivotal turn in 2009 when he achieved the coveted SCJP certification, solidifying his grasp of Java programming. But the following year, in 2010, he discovered his true calling: .NET development. This shift opened doors to exciting opportunities with various multinational corporations, both product-based and service-based.

Over the past 14 years, Nirbhay has honed his skills in a vast array of .NET technologies and Azure Cloud, including ASP.NET, C#, VB.NET, Web Forms, Win Forms, WPF, WCF, .NET Core, and SQL. His experience extends beyond coding, encompassing the successful migration of legacy applications to modern .NET frameworks. He's also played a key role in designing and architecting numerous desktop and web applications.

Nirbhay's passion extends far beyond his own expertise. He actively participates in the .NET developer community, giving and taking interviews, and even training aspiring developers eager to excel in this dynamic field. Driven by the motto "Life is teaching and I'm still learning," Nirbhay is a lifelong learner who thrives on sharing his knowledge. This zeal to connect with aspiring developers led him to create the popular YouTube channel "@DotNetInterviewCommunity," a valuable resource for anyone seeking to ace their .NET and/or Azure Cloud and/or Frontend job interview.

With his extensive experience, practical knowledge, and dedication to empowering others, Nirbhay Chauhan is the ideal guide to help you navigate the Frontend interview process with confidence. Let his insights in the "The Complete Front-End Interview Guide: Angular, Node.js, React, Next.js, Vue.js, & TypeScript" book be your key to unlocking your dream Frontent developer career.

PREVIEW OF MY BEST SELLING BOOKS

1. Master .NET Fundamentals

2. Master C# Interview Preparation

3. .NET Developer's Interview Toolkit

4. Mastering the .NET Core Interview

5. Conquer the Azure Developer Interview

6. The Complete Front-End Interview Guide

Why You Should Read "The Complete Front-End Interview Guide: Angular, Node.js, React, Next.js, Vue.js, & TypeScript"

Are you an Frontend developer looking to take your career to the next level? If so, then you need to read "The Complete Front-End Interview Guide". This comprehensive guide is your one-stop shop for mastering the essential concepts and skills required to ace your Frontend Developer interviews.

Here's why you should read this book:

- **Comprehensive Coverage:** This book covers a wide range of topics, including Angular, NodeJs, React, NextJs, VueJs and Typescript.

- **Structured Approach:** The book is organized in a logical and easy-to-follow manner, making it simple to understand and retain the information.
- **Practical Advice:** Throughout the book, you'll find practical advice and tips that will help you apply the concepts you learn to real-world interview questions.
- **Time-Saving:** By reading this book, you can save yourself the time and frustration of searching for information online and trying to organize your notes.
- **Digital Detox:** This physical book is a great alternative to spending hours in front of a computer screen, allowing you to study more comfortably and efficiently.

Whether you're a beginner or an experienced Frontend developer, this book is a valuable resource that will help you achieve your career goals. Don't miss out on this opportunity to level up your Azure skills and land your dream job.

Limits of Liability/Disclaimer of Warranty

The author and publisher have made their best efforts in preparing this book.

The author and publisher make no representations or warranties regarding the accuracy or completeness of the book's content.

The author and publisher specifically disclaim any implied warranties of merchantability or fitness for a particular purpose.

Warranties are limited to the descriptions contained in this paragraph and cannot be created or extended by sales representatives or written sales materials.

The accuracy, completeness, and opinions stated in the book are not guaranteed to produce particular results, and the advice and strategies may not be suitable for everyone.

The author shall be liable for any loss of profit or other commercial damages, including special, incidental, consequential, or other damages.

CONTENTS

Introduction: Your Path to Frontend Developer Interview Success

Are you an Frontend developer feeling overwhelmed by the sheer volume of information available online to prepare for interviews? Have you struggled to find a reliable source of questions and answers that truly reflect the challenges you'll face in real-world interviews?

I've been there myself. When I was preparing for my own Frontend developer interviews, I found myself lost in a sea of blog posts, tutorials, and forums. It was incredibly difficult to determine which resources were truly valuable and which were just noise. I spent countless hours bookmarking articles and trying to organize my notes, but it was a never-ending battle.

And let's not forget the pain of trying to find that one article you read weeks ago. Revisiting information online can be a time-consuming and frustrating process.

I knew there had to be a better way. A more structured, comprehensive approach that would equip me with the knowledge and confidence to ace any Frontend Developer interview. So, I embarked on a journey to create a collection of interview questions and answers. I poured over countless resources, analyzed past interview experiences, and distilled the most essential concepts into a cohesive framework.

The result is this book, "The Complete Front-End Interview Guide: Angular, Node.js, React, Next.js, Vue.js, & TypeScript". It's not just a collection of questions; it's a roadmap to your Frontend Developer interview success. Each chapter is designed to provide you with a deep understanding of the core concepts and technologies that are essential for Frontend developers, this book covers everything you need to know.

But this book offers more than just content. It's a solution to the constant struggle of finding and revisiting information online. With this book, you have all the essential knowledge at your fingertips, ready to be reviewed whenever you need it.

Additionally, in an age of digital detox, this book provides a much-needed respite from screen time. Instead of straining your eyes in front of a computer or mobile device, you can simply pick up this physical book and start studying.

By addressing these common pain points, this book offers a win-win solution for aspiring Frontend developers. It provides a

comprehensive resource, eliminates the frustration of searching
for information online, and promotes a healthier work-life
balance.

CHAPTER 1

—•—

ANGULAR

What is Angular?

Angular is a powerful, open-source JavaScript framework developed and maintained by Google. It's primarily used to build dynamic, single-page web applications.

Key Features:

- **Component-Based Architecture:** Breaks down applications into reusable components, making code modular and maintainable.

- **TypeScript:** Uses TypeScript, a superset of JavaScript, for strong typing and better code structure.

- **Two-Way Data Binding:** Automatically synchronizes data between the model and the view.

- **Dependency Injection:** Manages dependencies between components and services.

- **Routing:** Enables navigation between different views within an application.

- **Templating:** Uses a declarative template syntax to create user interfaces.

- **Forms:** Provides built-in form validation and data binding.

- **HTTP Client:** Makes HTTP requests to communicate with backend services.

- **Reactive Programming:** Leverages RxJS for handling asynchronous operations and data streams.

Benefits of Using Angular:

- **Improved Code Quality:** TypeScript enforces type safety, reducing errors and improving code readability.

- **Enhanced Developer Productivity:** The framework provides a structured approach to development and includes a rich set of tools and libraries.

- **Scalability:** Angular is well-suited for building large-scale applications.

- **Strong Community Support:** A large and active community provides extensive documentation, tutorials, and support.

- **Performance Optimization:** Built-in performance optimization techniques like change detection and lazy loading.

Evolution of Angular

Angular has undergone significant evolution since its inception. Here's a brief overview of its key versions and advancements:

ANGULAR

AngularJS (Angular 1.x) Released in 2010

- **JavaScript Framework:** Built on JavaScript, AngularJS was a popular choice for building dynamic web applications.

- **MVC Architecture:** Adhered to the Model-View-Controller architectural pattern.

- **Two-Way Data Binding:** Automatically synchronized data between the model and the view.

- **Directives:** Custom HTML attributes and elements to extend HTML's capabilities.

Angular 2+ (Modern Angular) Released in 2016

- **TypeScript:** Adopted TypeScript for improved code quality and maintainability.

- **Component-Based Architecture:** Focused on building reusable components.

- **Improved Performance:** Enhanced performance through Ahead-of-Time (AOT) compilation and change detection optimizations.

- **Mobile Development:** Supported mobile development through frameworks like Ionic.

- **Ivy Renderer:** Introduced a new rendering engine for faster rendering and smaller bundle sizes.

Key Versions and Their Contributions:

- **Angular 2:** The foundational version, introducing the modern framework.

- **Angular 4 (2017):** Focused on performance improvements, reduced bundle size, and simplified development.

- **Angular 5 (2017):** Introduced build optimizer, improved type checking, and added support for server-side rendering (SSR).

- **Angular 6 (2018):** Introduced the ng update command for easier updates, improved CLI, and support for RxJS 6.

- **Angular 7 (2018):** Improved performance, introduced virtual scrolling, and added support for drag-and-drop.

- **Angular 8 (2019):** Introduced differential loading, Ivy renderer by default, and improved performance.

- **Angular 9 (2020):** Enhanced performance, introduced Ivy rendering engine by default, and improved build times.

- **Angular 10 (2020):** Improved performance, introduced strict mode, and added new features like date range picker and form validation.

- **Angular 11 (2021):** Introduced lazy loading by route, improved performance, and added support for Web Workers.

- **Angular 12 (2021):** Focused on performance improvements, reduced bundle size, and introduced new language service features.

- **Angular 13 (2023):** Improved performance, introduced standalone components, and simplified the development experience.

- **Angular 14 (2023):** Introduced standalone components, enhanced performance, and improved developer experience.

- **Angular 15 (2023):** Introduced stable standalone APIs, improved performance, and enhanced developer experience.

What are the key differences between AngularJS and Angular?

While both AngularJS and Angular are JavaScript frameworks developed by Google, they have significant differences in architecture, performance, and development approach:

Architecture

- **AngularJS:** Uses a Model-View-Controller (MVC) architecture, where the application is divided into three main parts: Model, View, and Controller.

- **Angular:** Employs a component-based architecture, breaking down the application into reusable components.

Language

- **AngularJS:** Uses JavaScript.

- **Angular:** Uses TypeScript, a superset of JavaScript that provides type safety and other features.

Data Binding

- **AngularJS:** Primarily uses two-way data binding, which automatically synchronizes data between the model and the view.

- **Angular:** Supports both one-way and two-way data binding, providing more flexibility and control over data flow.

Performance

- **Angular:** Offers better performance due to its component-based architecture, change detection optimization, and Ahead-of-Time (AOT) compilation.

- **AngularJS:** Can suffer from performance issues, especially in large-scale applications, due to its digest cycle and two-way data binding.

Mobile Development

- **Angular:** Provides strong support for mobile development through frameworks like Ionic.

- **AngularJS:** While possible, mobile development with AngularJS is not as seamless as with Angular.

Development Experience

- **Angular:** Offers a more structured and scalable development experience with features like dependency injection, modularity, and a robust CLI.

- **AngularJS:** Can be more forgiving for beginners but may become complex for large-scale applications.

In summary, Angular is a significant improvement over AngularJS, offering better performance, scalability, and a more modern development experience. While AngularJS may still be used for legacy applications, Angular is the preferred choice for new projects.

Explain the concept of data binding in Angular.

Data binding in Angular is a powerful mechanism that automatically synchronizes data between the component's model and the view (the DOM). This means that changes made to the model are reflected in the view, and vice versa.

Types of Data Binding in Angular:

1. **Interpolation:**

   - One-way data binding from the component to the view.

   - Uses double curly braces {{ }} to display component properties in the template.

<p>Hello, {{ name }}!</p>

2. **Property Binding:**

   - One-way data binding from the component to the view.

   - Uses square brackets [] to bind component properties to HTML attributes.

<input [value]="name">

3. **Event Binding:**

   - One-way data binding from the view to the component.

   - Uses parentheses () to bind DOM events to component methods.

```
<button (click)="onClick()">Click me</button>
```

4. **Two-Way Data Binding:**

   - Combines interpolation and event binding for bidirectional data flow.

   - Uses [(ngModel)] syntax to bind component properties to form controls.

```
<input [(ngModel)]="name">
```

How Data Binding Works:

1. **Change Detection:** Angular's change detection mechanism monitors the component's data for changes.

2. **DOM Update:** When a change is detected, Angular updates the DOM to reflect the new data.

3. **Event Handling:** User interactions with the view trigger events, which are handled by the component's methods.

4. **Model Update:** The component's methods update the model data, triggering another change detection cycle.

Benefits of Data Binding:

- **Simplified Development:** Reduces the amount of manual DOM manipulation.

- **Improved Code Readability:** Makes code more concise and easier to understand.

- **Enhanced User Experience:** Enables dynamic and responsive user interfaces.

What is the difference between interpolation and property binding?

Key Differences between interpolation and property binding:

Feature	Interpolation	Property Binding
Purpose	Displaying data directly in the template	Setting DOM element properties
Syntax	{{ expression }}	[property]="expression"
Data Type	Always converts to a string	Can bind various data types (strings, numbers, booleans, objects, etc.)
Flexibility	Less flexible, primarily for simple data display	More flexible, can be used for complex scenarios like conditional rendering and dynamic styling

When to Use Which:

- **Interpolation:** Use for simple data display, like names, dates, or short text snippets.

- **Property Binding:** Use for more complex scenarios, such as:

    - Setting dynamic attributes (e.g., [class], [style])

    - Binding to non-string properties (e.g., [disabled], [hidden])

    - Creating dynamic HTML structures

Explain the concept of change detection in Angular.

Change detection is a core mechanism in Angular that keeps the view synchronized with the model. When data in a component changes, Angular's change detection system detects these changes and updates the DOM accordingly.

How it Works:

1. **Initial Rendering:**

    - When a component is initialized, Angular performs an initial change detection cycle.

    - It checks the component's properties and expressions.

    - It renders the template based on the initial values.

2. **Change Detection Trigger:**

   ○ Change detection can be triggered by various events:

     - User interactions (e.g., clicks, input changes)

     - HTTP requests

     - Timers

     - Programmatic changes to component properties

3. **Change Detection Cycle:**

   ○ Angular starts a new change detection cycle.

   ○ It checks for changes in the component's properties and expressions.

   ○ If changes are detected:

     - Angular updates the DOM to reflect the new values.

     - The process continues until no more changes are found.

Change Detection Strategies:

Angular offers two primary change detection strategies:

1. **Default Strategy (OnPush):**

   ○ Components with the OnPush change detection strategy only trigger a change detection cycle when:

- Input properties change.

- Observable streams emit new values.

- Explicitly triggered by calling markForCheck().

○ This strategy can improve performance by reducing unnecessary change detection cycles.

2. **Default Strategy (Default):**

○ Components without the OnPush strategy trigger a change detection cycle whenever any change occurs within the component or its child components.

○ This strategy is simpler to implement but can lead to performance issues in large applications with frequent changes.

Best Practices for Efficient Change Detection:

- **Use OnPush Strategy:** Employ the OnPush strategy whenever possible to optimize performance.

- **Minimize Change Detection Triggers:** Avoid unnecessary triggers, such as frequent property changes or unnecessary HTTP requests.

- **Use Immutable Data Structures:** Immutable data structures can help Angular detect changes more efficiently.

- **Optimize Template Expressions:** Write efficient template expressions to reduce the amount of work Angular needs to do during change detection.

- **Use markForCheck() Judiciously:** Use markForCheck() only when necessary to trigger change detection for specific components.

What is the difference between ngOnChanges, ngOnInit, and ngAfterViewInit lifecycle hooks?

Angular provides a set of lifecycle hooks that allow you to execute specific code at different stages of a component's lifecycle. Let's delve into three of the most commonly used hooks: ngOnChanges, ngOnInit, and ngAfterViewInit.

1. ngOnChanges

- **Triggered:** Whenever input properties of a component change.

- **Purpose:**
    - To react to changes in input properties.
    - To perform actions based on the new values of the input properties.

- **Common Use Cases:**
    - Updating the component's state or view based on the new input values.
    - Fetching data from a service using the new input values.
    - Performing calculations or transformations on the input values.

2. ngOnInit

- **Triggered:** Once, after the component is initialized and its inputs are set.

- **Purpose:**

    - To perform initialization tasks that only need to be done once.

    - To subscribe to observables.

    - To fetch data from a service.

3. ngAfterViewInit

- **Triggered:** After Angular initializes the component's view and its child views.

- **Purpose:**

    - To access and manipulate the DOM elements of the component and its children.

    - To set up event listeners.

    - To initialize third-party libraries that rely on the DOM.

Key Differences Summarized:

Hook	Triggered	Purpose
ngOnChanges	Input property changes	React to input property changes
ngOnInit	After initialization	Perform initial setup tasks
ngAfterViewInit	After view initialization	Access and manipulate the DOM

Example:

TypeScript

```
@Component({

selector: 'app-my-component',

template: ` <p>Name: {{ name }}</p>

<div #myDiv>Hello, World!</div> `

})

export class MyComponent implements OnInit, AfterViewInit, OnChanges {

@Input() name: string;

constructor() { }

ngOnChanges(changes: SimpleChanges) {
```

```
console.log('ngOnChanges', changes);

}

ngOnInit() {

console.log('ngOnInit');

// Fetch data, subscribe to observables, etc.

}

ngAfterViewInit() {

console.log('ngAfterViewInit');

// Access DOM elements, e.g.,

const myDiv = this.myDiv.nativeElement;

myDiv.style.color = 'blue';

}

}
```

What is the difference between async and promise in Angular?

While both async/await and **Promises** are mechanisms to handle asynchronous operations in Angular, they differ in their syntax and approach:

Promises

- **Object-based:** A Promise is an object representing the eventual completion (or failure) of an asynchronous operation.

- **Chaining:** Promises can be chained using .then() and .catch() methods to handle successful and failed outcomes.

- **Syntax:** Can be verbose and prone to callback hell, especially when chaining multiple operations.

Example:

JavaScript

```javascript
fetch('https://api.example.com/data')

.then(response => response.json())

.then(data => console.log(data))

.catch(error => console.error(error));
```

Async/Await

- **Syntactic Sugar:** A cleaner syntax built on top of Promises.

- **Synchronous-like:** It allows you to write asynchronous code in a synchronous-like style using the async and await keywords.

- **Readability:** Makes asynchronous code more readable and easier to understand.

Example:

JavaScript

```javascript
async function fetchData() {

try {
```

```
const response = await fetch('https://api.example.com/data');

const data = await response.json();

console.log(data);

} catch (error) {  console.error(error);  }}
```

Key Differences:

Feature	Promises	Async/Await
Syntax	Chaining .then() and .catch()	async and await keywords
Readability	Can be less readable, especially with nested callbacks	More readable, closer to synchronous code
Error Handling	Requires explicit error handling with .catch()	Uses try...catch blocks

When to Use Which:

Promises:

- When you need more flexibility and control over asynchronous operations.

- When you're working with older JavaScript environments that don't fully support async/await.

Async/Await:

- For most modern Angular applications, async/await is preferred due to its improved readability and ease of use.

- When you want to write asynchronous code in a more synchronous style.

Explain the concept of RxJS and its role in Angular.

RxJS (Reactive Extensions for JavaScript) is a powerful library for composing asynchronous and event-based programs using observable sequences. It provides a functional programming approach to handle data streams over time.

Why RxJS in Angular?

- **Asynchronous Operations:** Angular heavily relies on asynchronous operations like HTTP requests, timers, and user interactions. RxJS provides a robust way to handle these operations and manage data streams efficiently.

- **Event Handling:** RxJS simplifies event handling by treating events as observable streams. This makes it easier to combine multiple event streams, filter events, and react to changes in real-time.

- **Data Flow:** RxJS promotes a declarative style of programming, where you define how data should flow through your application rather than explicitly managing state changes.

Core Concepts in RxJS:

- **Observable:** Represents a stream of data or events over time.

- **Observer:** Subscribes to an observable and receives notifications (next, error, complete) as data is emitted.

- **Operator:** A function that transforms an observable stream, creating a new observable with modified data.

- **Subject:** A special type of observable that allows both subscribing and emitting values.

Common RxJS Operators in Angular:

- **map:** Transforms the values of an observable.

- **filter:** Filters values based on a condition.

- **switchMap:** Cancels previous inner observables and subscribes to a new one.

- **mergeMap:** Concatenates multiple inner observables.

- **debounceTime:** Delays the emission of values until a certain time has passed.

Example: Using RxJS to Fetch Data in Angular

TypeScript

```typescript
import { Component, OnInit } from '@angular/core';

import { HttpClient } from '@angular/common/http';

import { Observable } from 'rxjs';

@Component({
```

```
selector:

'app-my-component',

template: `  <div *ngIf="data$ | async as data">

{{ data.name }}   </div> `

})

export class MyComponent implements OnInit {

data$: Observable<any>;

constructor(private http: HttpClient) {}

ngOnInit() {

this.data$ = this.http.get('https://api.example.com/data')

.pipe( map(response => response.json()) );

}

}
```

In this example, we use HttpClient to fetch data from an API. The map operator is used to transform the HTTP response into JSON format. The async pipe in the template automatically subscribes to the data$ observable and updates the view whenever new data is emitted.

What are observables and how are they used in Angular?

Observables are a powerful concept in RxJS, and they play a crucial role in Angular's reactive programming paradigm. They represent a stream of data or events over time.

Key Concepts:

- **Observable:** A source of data that emits values over time.

- **Observer:** Subscribes to an observable and receives notifications (next, error, complete) as data is emitted.

- **Subscription:** A handle to the subscription, allowing you to unsubscribe from the observable.

How Observables Are Used in Angular:

1. **Handling Asynchronous Operations:**

   - **HTTP Requests:** Angular's HttpClient returns observables, allowing you to handle network requests asynchronously.

   - **Timers:** You can create observables to emit values at specific intervals.

   - **User Events:** You can convert DOM events (e.g., clicks, keystrokes) into observables.

2. **Managing Data Streams:**

   - **Real-time Data:** Observables are ideal for handling real-time data streams, such as WebSocket feeds or server-sent events.

   - **Data Transformations:** You can use RxJS operators to transform and filter data streams.

3. **Component Communication:**

- **Parent-Child Communication:** You can use observables to pass data from a parent component to a child component.

- **Sibling Communication:** Observables can be used to share data between sibling components.

Example: Using Observables to Fetch Data

TypeScript

```typescript
import { Component, OnInit } from '@angular/core';

import { HttpClient } from '@angular/common/http';

@Component({

selector: 'app-my-component',

template: `  <div *ngIf="data$ | async as data">

{{ data.name }}   </div> `

})

export class MyComponent implements OnInit {

data$: Observable<any>;

constructor(private http: HttpClient) {}

ngOnInit() {

this.data$ = this.http.get('https://api.example.com/data')

.pipe( map(response => response.json()) );

}
```

}

Explanation:

1. The HttpClient.get() method returns an observable.

2. The map operator transforms the HTTP response into JSON data.

3. The async pipe in the template subscribes to the data$ observable and updates the view whenever new data is emitted.

Benefits of Using Observables in Angular:

- **Reactive Programming:** Observables promote a reactive programming style, making your code more responsive to changes.

- **Asynchronous Operations:** They provide a clean and efficient way to handle asynchronous operations.

- **Data Streams:** You can easily work with data streams, filter, transform, and combine them as needed.

- **Error Handling:** Observables offer robust error handling mechanisms.

What is the difference between subscribe and pipe operators in RxJS?

In RxJS, subscribe and pipe are two essential operators, but they serve distinct purposes in handling and transforming observable streams.

Subscribe

- **Purpose:** Subscribes to an observable and defines callbacks for handling emitted values, errors, and completion.

- **Action:** Activates the observable, triggering the emission of values.

- **Side Effects:** Typically used for side effects, such as updating the DOM, logging, or making API calls.

Example:

TypeScript

```
const myObservable = interval(1000);
```

```
myObservable.subscribe(

value => console.log(value),

error => console.error(error),

() => console.log('Completed')

);
```

Pipe

- **Purpose:** Chains a series of operators to transform an observable stream.

- **Action:** Returns a new observable, applying the specified operators to its values.

- **Pure Function:** Does not trigger the observable's execution.

Example:

TypeScript

```
const myObservable = interval(1000);


const transformedObservable = myObservable.pipe(

map(value => value * 2),

filter(value => value % 2 === 0)

);

transformedObservable.subscribe(value => console.log(value));
```

Key Differences:

Feature	Subscribe	Pipe
Purpose	Activates the observable and handles emissions	Transforms and manipulates the observable stream
Return Value	Subscription object	New observable
Side Effects	Typically used for side effects	Pure function, no side effects
Timing	Immediately triggers the observable	Doesn't trigger until subscribed to

Best Practices:

- **Avoid Over-Subscribing:** Unsubscribe from observables when they are no longer needed to prevent memory leaks.

- **Use async Pipe in Angular Templates:** For simple scenarios, the async pipe can handle subscriptions and unsubscriptions automatically.

- **Use pipe for Complex Transformations:** For complex transformations, pipe allows you to chain multiple operators in a readable and efficient way.

Explain the role of components in Angular.

In Angular, components are the fundamental building blocks of user interfaces. They encapsulate a specific part of the UI, along with its associated logic and data. Think of them as self-contained modules that can be reused across your application.

Key Roles of Components:

1. **Encapsulation:**

   - Components isolate their internal logic and data from the rest of the application. This promotes modularity and maintainability.

   - Changes made within a component don't affect other components unless explicitly communicated through input and output properties.

2. **Reusability:**

   - Well-designed components can be reused in multiple parts of your application, reducing code duplication and improving consistency.

   - You can even create custom components that can be shared across different projects.

3. **Modularity:**

   - Components break down complex UIs into smaller, manageable parts.

   - This makes it easier to understand, test, and update your application.

4. Data Binding:

- ○ Components use data binding to communicate with each other and the parent component.

- ○ Input properties allow components to receive data from their parent components.

- ○ Output properties allow components to emit events and send data to their parent components.

Structure of an Angular Component:

- **Template:** Defines the HTML structure of the component's view.

- **Styles:** Contains CSS styles specific to the component.

- **TypeScript Class:** Implements the component's logic, including:

  - ○ Properties: Data that the component uses.

  - ○ Methods: Functions that perform actions within the component.

  - ○ Lifecycle Hooks: Methods that are called at different stages of the component's lifecycle.

Example:

TypeScript

```
@Component({

selector: 'app-product',
```

```
templateUrl: './product.component.html',

styleUrls: ['./product.component.css']

})

export class ProductComponent {

@Input() product:Product;


addToCart() {

// Add product to cart logic

}

}
```

In this example:

- The ProductComponent is defined with a selector app-product.

- It receives a product object as input.

- The template defines the HTML structure of the product card.

- The addToCart() method is called when the "Add to Cart" button is clicked.

What is the difference between a component and a directive?

While both components and directives are fundamental building blocks in Angular, they have distinct roles and characteristics:

ANGULAR

Components

- **Encapsulated UI units:** Components are self-contained units of UI that encapsulate their own template, styles, and logic.

- **Own View:** Each component has its own view, defined by its template.

- **Reusability:** Components can be reused across different parts of an application, promoting modularity and code reusability.

- **Data Binding:** Components can bind data to their templates and communicate with other components using input and output properties.

- **Lifecycle Hooks:** Components have lifecycle hooks that allow you to perform actions at different stages of their lifecycle, such as initialization, change detection, and destruction.

Directives

- **Behavior Modifiers:** Directives are used to modify the behavior or appearance of existing DOM elements.

- **No Own View:** Directives don't have their own view; they are applied to existing elements.

- **Types of Directives:**

  - **Attribute Directives:** Modify the appearance or behavior of an element. (e.g., ngClass, ngStyle)

○ **Structural Directives:** Modify the DOM structure by adding or removing elements. (e.g., *ngIf, *ngFor)

Key Differences

Feature	Component	Directive
Purpose	Encapsulate UI and logic	Modify behavior or appearance of DOM elements
View	Has its own view (template)	No own view
Reusability	Highly reusable	Less reusable, often used for specific modifications
Lifecycle Hooks	Has lifecycle hooks	No lifecycle hooks (unless used with @Directive)

In essence:

- **Components** are like self-contained widgets that you can plug into your application.

- **Directives** are tools to modify the behavior or appearance of existing elements.

What are the key properties of a component?

In Angular, components are the fundamental building blocks of user interfaces. They encapsulate a specific part of the UI, along with its associated logic and data. Key properties of a component include:

1. **Selector:**

    - A unique identifier used to select the component in a template.

    - Determines where the component's template will be inserted in the parent component's template.

2. **Template:**

    - Defines the HTML structure of the component's view.

    - Can contain HTML elements, Angular directives, and component instances.

3. **Styles:**

    - Contains CSS styles specific to the component.

    - Can be used to customize the appearance of the component's view.

4. **TypeScript Class:** Implements the component's logic, including:

    - **Properties:** Data that the component uses.

    - **Methods:** Functions that perform actions within the component.

    - **Lifecycle Hooks:** Methods that are called at different stages of the component's lifecycle.

5. **Input Properties:**

- Allow data to be passed from a parent component to the child component.

- Decorated with the @Input() decorator.

6. **Output Properties:**

- Allow the child component to emit events and data to the parent component.

- Decorated with the @Output() decorator.

How do you create a new component in Angular?

Here's a step-by-step guide on how to create a new component in an Angular application:

1. Generate the Component:

You can use the Angular CLI to generate a new component. Open your terminal and navigate to your Angular project's root directory. Then, run the following command:

Bash

ng generate component component-name

Replace component-name with the desired name for your component. This command will create a new directory with the following files:

- **component-name.component.ts:** The TypeScript file containing the component's logic.

- **component-name.component.html:** The template file for the component's view.

- **component-name.component.css:** The CSS file for the component's styles.

- **component-name.component.spec.ts:** The test file for the component.

2. Import and Declare the Component:

- **Import:** Import the generated component in your app.module.ts file.

- **Declare:** Add the component to the declarations array in the @NgModule decorator.

TypeScript

// app.module.ts

import { NgModule } from '@angular/core';

import { BrowserModule } from '@angular/platform-browser';

import { AppComponent } from './app.component';

import { ComponentNameComponent } from './component-name/component-name.component'; // Import

the new component

@NgModule({

declarations: [

```
AppComponent,

ComponentNameComponent // Declare the new component

],

imports: [

BrowserModule

],

providers: [],

bootstrap: [AppComponent]

})

export class AppModule { }
```

3. Use the Component in a Template:

You can now use the component in your templates by using its selector. For example, if the selector of your component is app-component-name, you can use it like this:

HTML

```
<app-component-name></app-component-name>
```

4. Implement Component Logic:

In the component-name.component.ts file, you can define:

- **Properties:** Data that the component uses.

- **Methods:** Functions that perform actions within the component.

- **Lifecycle Hooks:** Methods that are called at different stages of the component's lifecycle (e.g., ngOnInit, ngOnChanges, ngOnDestroy).

TypeScript

```
// component-name.component.ts

@Component({

selector: 'app-component-name',

templateUrl: './component-name.component.html',

styleUrls: ['./component-name.component.css']

})

export class ComponentNameComponent

{

// Component properties and methods

}
```

Explain the role of templates in Angular.

In Angular, templates serve as the blueprint for the user interface (UI) within a component. They define how the component's data is displayed and how user interactions are handled.

Key Roles of Templates in Angular:

1. **Data Binding:**

   - **Interpolation:** Displays component data within the template using double curly braces {{ }}.

   - **Property Binding:** Sets properties of HTML elements to component properties using square brackets [].

   - **Event Binding:** Handles user events (like clicks) and binds them to component methods using parentheses ().

2. **Structural Directives:** Control the DOM structure by adding, removing, or manipulating elements based on conditions. Examples: *ngIf, *ngFor, *ngSwitch.

3. **Attribute Directives:** Change the appearance or behavior of an element. Examples: ngClass, ngStyle, [disabled].

4. **Component Interaction:** Templates can include other components, creating a hierarchical structure. Data can be passed between parent and child components using @Input and @Output.

Example:

HTML

```
<div>

<h2>{{ title }}</h2>
```

```
<ul>

<li *ngFor="let hero of heroes">

{{ hero.name }}

</li>

</ul>

</div>
```

What are the different types of templates in Angular?

In Angular, while there isn't a strict categorization into distinct "types" of templates, the way they are defined and used can be broadly classified:

1. **Inline Templates:** Defined directly within the @Component decorator using the template property.

Example:

TypeScript

```
@Component({

selector: 'app-my-component',

template: `

<h1>{{ title }}</h1>

<p>This is an inline template.</p> `

})

export class MyComponent {
```

title = 'My Component';

}

Use Cases: Suitable for small, simple components with a concise template.

2. External Templates: Defined in a separate HTML file and linked to the component using the templateUrl property in the @Component decorator.

Example:

Component (my-component.component.ts):
```
 TypeScript
@Component({

selector: 'app-my-component',

templateUrl: './my-component.component.html'

})

export class MyComponent {

// ...

}
```

Template (my-component.component.html):
```
 HTML
<h1>{{ title }}</h1>

<p>This is an external template.</p>
```

Use Cases: Preferred for larger, more complex components with extensive templates, as it promotes better code organization and readability.

3. Template URLs: Similar to external templates, but the template file is located in a different directory from the component file.

Example:

Component (my-component.component.ts):
```typescript
TypeScript
@Component({

selector: 'app-my-component',

templateUrl: '../templates/my-component.html'

})

export class MyComponent {

// ...

}
```

Template (templates/my-component.html):
```html
HTML
<h1>{{ title }}</h1>

<p>This is a template with a custom URL.</p>
```

Use Cases: Useful for organizing templates into a dedicated directory for better project structure.

How do you pass data from a parent component to a child component and vice versa?

Passing Data from Parent to Child Component in Angular

@Input() Decorator:

- The parent component defines a property decorated with @Input().

- The child component binds to this property using the property binding syntax ([]).

Example:

Parent Component:
TypeScript
import { Component } from '@angular/core';

@Component({

selector: 'app-parent',

template: `

<app-child [name]="parentName"></app-child> ` })

export class ParentComponent { parentName = 'Parent'; }

Child Component:
TypeScript
import { Component, Input } from '@angular/core';

```
@Component({

selector: 'app-child',

template: ` <p>Hello, {{ name }}!</p> `

})

export class ChildComponent { @Input() name: string = ''; }
```

Using a Service:

- Create a service to hold the data.

- Inject the service into both parent and child components.

- The parent component updates the data in the service.

- The child component subscribes to changes in the service and updates its own data accordingly.

Passing Data from Child to Parent Component in Angular

@Output() and EventEmitter:

1. The child component defines an EventEmitter and decorates it with @Output().

2. The child component emits an event with the data using the emit() method.

3. The parent component listens to this event using the event binding syntax (()).

Example:
Child Component:

```typescript
TypeScript
import { Component, Output, EventEmitter } from
'@angular/core';


@Component({

selector: 'app-child',

template: `

<button (click)="sendValue()">Send Value</button> `

})

export class ChildComponent {

@Output() valueChanged = new EventEmitter<string>();


sendValue() { this.valueChanged.emit('Value from Child'); }

}
```

Parent Component:

```typescript
TypeScript
import { Component } from '@angular/core';


@Component({

selector: 'app-parent',
```

```
template: ` <app-child
(valueChanged)="onValueChanged($event)"></app-child>

<p>Value from Child: {{ childValue }}</p> `

})

export class ParentComponent {

childValue = '';

onValueChanged(value: string) { this.childValue = value; }

}
```

What is content projection and how is it used?

Content Projection in Angular allows you to pass content from a parent component into the template of a child component.

How it Works:

- **<ng-content>**: The child component's template uses the <ng-content> tag to define the placeholder where the projected content will be inserted.

- **Parent Component:** The parent component places the content that it wants to project within the child component's tag.

Example:

Child Component (my-component.component.ts):

TypeScript

```typescript
import { Component } from '@angular/core';


@Component({

selector: 'app-my-component',

template: `  <div>

<h2>Child Component</h2>

<ng-content></ng-content>

</div>  ` })
export class MyComponent {  // ... }
```

Parent Component (parent.component.ts):

TypeScript

```typescript
import { Component } from '@angular/core';


@Component({

selector: 'app-parent',

template: `  <app-my-component>

<h3>Projected Content from Parent</h3>
```

```
<p>This content is projected into the child component.</p>

</app-my-component> ` })
```

export class ParentComponent { // ... }

In this example:

- The MyComponent (child) has an <ng-content> tag in its template.

- The ParentComponent places the <h3> and <p> tags within the app-my-component tag. This content will be projected into the <ng-content> placeholder in the child component's template.

Use Cases:

- **Creating reusable components:** Content projection allows you to create reusable components with flexible content. For example, a generic Alert component can be created to display different types of messages.

- **Customizing component behavior:** You can allow users to customize the child component's behavior by injecting their own content.

- **Improving component flexibility:** Content projection makes components more adaptable and reusable by allowing for different content to be displayed within them.

Key Considerations:

- **Multiple <ng-content> Tags:** You can use multiple <ng-content> tags with different select attributes to project content to specific locations within the child component's template.

- **Content Projection and Selectors:** You can use selectors with <ng-content> to project only specific types of content (e.g., <ng-content select=".my-class">).

What is the purpose of services in Angular?

In Angular, **services** are a crucial architectural concept that promote code reusability, maintainability, and testability. They encapsulate specific functionalities or data that can be shared across different parts of your application.

Key Purposes of Services in Angular:

1. **Data Sharing:**

   - Services can hold and manage application-wide data, such as user preferences, authentication tokens, or application settings.

   - Components can easily access and share this data through the service.

2. **Business Logic:**

   - Encapsulate complex business logic or calculations within a service.

   - This keeps your components lean and focused on presentation and user interaction.

3. **Data Access:**

  ○ Services are responsible for interacting with external data sources like APIs, databases, or local storage.

  ○ Components can then use the service to fetch or save data without dealing with the underlying data access mechanisms.

4. **Side Effects:**

  ○ Handle side effects like HTTP requests, subscriptions, or timers within a service.

  ○ This helps to isolate these operations and make your components more predictable and easier to test.

5. **Third-Party Integrations:**

  ○ Integrate with third-party libraries or APIs through services.

  ○ This centralizes the integration logic and makes it easier to manage and update.

Example:

Imagine an e-commerce application. You might have a ProductService that:

- Fetches product data from an API.

- Handles product filtering and sorting.

- Manages the shopping cart.

Key Benefits of Using Services:

- **Improved Code Organization:** Services promote better code organization and modularity.

- **Increased Reusability:** Services can be easily reused across multiple components.

- **Enhanced Testability:** Services are easier to unit test in isolation from components.

- **Improved Maintainability:** Changes to data access or business logic can be made in one place and easily reflected throughout the application.

How do you create a service in Angular?

1. Create a Service Class:

Generate a new service file using the Angular CLI:

```
Bashng generate service my-service
```

This command will create a file named my-service.service.ts in the src/app directory.

The generated service will look like this:

```
TypeScript
import { Injectable } from '@angular/core';
```

```
@Injectable({ providedIn: 'root' })

export class MyServiceService { constructor() { }}
```

2. Inject the Service into Components:

Import the service into the component:

```typescript
 TypeScript
import { Component } from '@angular/core';

import { MyServiceService } from './my-service.service';


@Component({

selector: 'app-my-component',

templateUrl: './my-component.component.html',

styleUrls: ['./my-component.component.css']

})


export class MyComponent {

constructor(private myService: MyServiceService) { }

dataFromService: string;

ngOnInit(): void {

this.dataFromService = this.myService.getData();

}}
```

Use the service's methods within the component:

- The constructor injects an instance of the MyServiceService into the component.

- You can now use the myService object to call the service's methods and access its data.

Explain the concept of dependency injection in Angular.

Dependency Injection is a core principle in Angular that promotes loose coupling and improves the testability and maintainability of your application.

Core Concepts:

- **Dependencies:** These are objects or services that a component needs to function correctly. For example, a component might depend on a data service to fetch data from an API.

- **Inversion of Control (IoC):** Instead of creating dependencies within a component, you "inject" them. Angular's dependency injection system is responsible for creating and providing the necessary dependencies to the component.

- **Injectors:** Angular maintains a hierarchy of injectors. The root injector is at the top, and child injectors are created for each component. Injectors are responsible for creating and providing instances of services.

How it Works:

Define Dependencies: In the component's constructor, you declare the dependencies you need by injecting them as parameters.

TypeScript
```typescript
constructor(private myService: MyService) { }
```

Angular's Role: When Angular creates an instance of the component, it also creates instances of the dependencies (in this case, MyService). Angular injects these dependencies into the component's constructor.

Using Dependencies: The component can now use the injected services to perform its tasks.

TypeScript
ngOnInit() { this.data = this.myService.getData(); }

What is the difference between providedIn: 'root' and providedIn: 'any'?

In Angular, the providedIn property within the @Injectable() decorator controls how a service is provided and shared across the application.

providedIn: 'root'

Scope: The service is provided at the root level of the application.

Behavior:

- A single instance of the service is created for the entire application.

- This instance is shared across all components, modules, and lazy-loaded modules.

Tree Shaking: Enables tree shaking, meaning that if a service is not used anywhere in the application, it can be removed from the final bundle, reducing the application's size.

When to Use:

- For services that need to be accessed and shared globally throughout the application.

- For services that manage application-wide state or data.

providedIn: 'any'

Scope: The service is provided at the module level.

Behavior:

- A new instance of the service is created for each module that injects it.

- Eagerly loaded modules share the same instance.

- Lazy-loaded modules each get their own unique instance.

Tree Shaking: Tree shaking is not as effective compared to providedIn: 'root' because the service might be included in the bundle even if it's not used in all modules.

When to Use:

- When you need to have different instances of the service in different modules.

- For services that manage module-specific data or logic.

Explain the different types of forms in Angular.

In Angular, there are two primary approaches to building forms:

1. Template-Driven Forms:

Approach: Relies heavily on HTML attributes and directives to define and manage form controls. Form logic is primarily defined within the HTML template.

Key Features: Uses directives like ngModel, ngForm, and ngSubmit. Simpler to implement for basic forms with straightforward validation. Good for smaller forms with minimal complexity.

Example:

HTML

```
<form #myForm="ngForm"
(ngSubmit)="onSubmit(myForm)">

<input type="text" name="name" ngModel required>

<button type="submit">Submit</button>

</form>
```

2. Reactive Forms:

Approach: Form controls are created programmatically within the component class. Provides more control and flexibility for complex forms.

Key Features: Uses classes like FormControl, FormGroup, and FormArray. Allows for complex validation logic within the component. Better suited for larger, more complex forms with intricate validation rules.

Example:

TypeScript

```typescript
import { Component } from '@angular/core';

import { FormGroup, FormControl, Validators } from '@angular/forms';


@Component({ // ... })

export class MyComponent {

myForm = new FormGroup({

name: new FormControl('', Validators.required),

email: new FormControl('', [Validators.required, Validators.email])

});


onSubmit() {

if (this.myForm.valid) {

// Handle form submission

}

}

}
```

Choosing the Right Approach:

- **Template-Driven:** Suitable for simple forms with basic validation and minimal logic.

- **Reactive:** Preferred for complex forms with intricate validation, dynamic form controls, and more advanced scenarios.

What are form controls and validators?

Form Controls

- **Foundation of Angular Forms:** In reactive forms, form controls are the building blocks. They represent individual input fields (like text boxes, checkboxes, etc.) within your form.

- **Types:**

  - FormControl: Represents a single input field.

  - FormGroup: Represents a collection of form controls, often used to group related fields (like an address form).

  - FormArray: Represents an array of form controls, useful for dynamic lists of inputs.

- **Key Properties:**

  - value: The current value of the control.

  - status: Indicates the validity of the control (VALID or INVALID).

  - errors: An object containing any validation errors associated with the control.

Validators

- **Enforce Rules:** Validators are functions that check the validity of a form control's value. They define the rules that the input must satisfy.

- **Built-in Validators:** Angular provides several built-in validators:

  - required: Ensures that the field is not empty.

  - minLength: Checks if the input string meets a minimum length.

  - maxLength: Checks if the input string meets a maximum length.

  - email: Validates email format.

  - pattern: Matches the input against a regular expression.

- **Custom Validators:** You can create your own custom validators to enforce specific business rules or complex validation logic.

Example:

TypeScript

```typescript
import { Component } from '@angular/core';

import { FormGroup, FormControl, Validators } from '@angular/forms';


@Component({ // ... })
```

```
export class MyComponent {

myForm = new FormGroup({

name: new FormControl('', Validators.required),

email: new FormControl('', [Validators.required,
Validators.email])

});

// ... }
```

What is an Angular Router?

Angular Router is a powerful feature within the Angular framework that enables navigation between different views within a single-page application (SPA). It allows you to define routes that map URLs to specific components, creating a seamless user experience without the need for full page reloads.

Key Concepts:

- **Routes:** These are JavaScript objects that define a path and the component that should be displayed for that path.

- **Router Outlet:** This is a directive (<router-outlet>) that acts as a placeholder in your template. The router dynamically inserts the component associated with the current route into this outlet.

- **Navigation:** Users can navigate between routes by:

    - Clicking on links with the routerLink directive.

    - Programmatically navigating using the Router service.

○ Changing the URL directly in the browser's address bar.

Example:

1. Define Routes:

TypeScript

```
import { Routes } from '@angular/router';


const routes: Routes = [

{ path: '', component: HomeComponent },

{ path: 'about', component: AboutComponent },

{ path: 'products', component: ProductsComponent } ];
```

2. Import and Configure Router:

TypeScript

```
import { BrowserModule } from '@angular/platform-browser';

import { NgModule } from '@angular/core';

import { RouterModule, Routes } from '@angular/router';


// ... your routes


@NgModule({
```

```
imports: [   BrowserModule,

RouterModule.forRoot(routes)

], // ... })

export class AppModule { }
```

3. Create Links:

HTML

```html
<a routerLink="/">Home</a>

<a routerLink="/about">About</a>

<a routerLink="/products">Products</a>
```

4. Add Router Outlet:

HTML

```html
<router-outlet></router-outlet>
```

Key Benefits:

- **Single-Page Application Experience:** Provides a smooth and responsive user experience without full page reloads.

- **Improved User Interface:** Enables complex navigation structures and deep linking within your application.

- **Better Organization:** Helps to organize your application into modular components based on routes.

- **SEO:** Angular Router can be configured to work well with search engine optimization (SEO).

What is Eager and Lazy loading in Angular?

In Angular, loading modules can significantly impact your application's performance. Eager and Lazy loading are two strategies for loading modules:

1. Eager Loading:

- **How it works:**

    - All modules are loaded initially when the application starts.

    - Modules are included in the initial bundle, regardless of whether they are immediately needed.

- **Pros:** Simple to implement.

- **Cons:** Can result in larger initial bundle sizes, leading to slower initial load times. May load unnecessary modules, impacting performance.

Example: Eager Loading:

TypeScript

const routes: Routes = [

{ path: '', component: HomeComponent },

{ path: 'about', component: AboutComponent },

{ path: 'products', component: ProductsComponent }];

2. Lazy Loading:

How it works: Modules are loaded only when they are needed. Modules are loaded dynamically using the loadChildren property in the Routes configuration.

Pros:

- Reduces initial bundle size, leading to faster initial load times.

- Improves performance by only loading necessary modules.

- Better user experience, especially for large applications with many features.

Cons:

- Can introduce some complexity in the routing configuration.

- May have a slight delay when lazy-loaded modules are first accessed.

Example: Lazy Loading:

TypeScript

```typescript
const routes: Routes = [

{ path: ", component: HomeComponent },

{ path: 'about', component: AboutComponent },

{ path: 'products', loadChildren: () =>
import('./products/products.module').then(m =>
m.ProductsModule) } ];
```

Key Differences:

- **Eager Loading:** The products module is loaded along with the initial application bundle.

- **Lazy Loading:** The products module is only loaded when the user navigates to the /products route.

What is AOT compilation? What are the advantages of AOT?

AOT (Ahead-of-Time) Compilation in Angular refers to the process of compiling your Angular application's HTML templates and TypeScript code into efficient JavaScript code **before** the browser downloads and executes it.

Here's how it works:

1. **During the build process:** The AOT compiler analyzes your application's components, templates, and metadata.

2. **It converts:** Angular-specific syntax (like data binding, directives) into plain JavaScript code.

3. **The browser receives:** Pre-compiled JavaScript code, ready to be executed immediately.

Key Advantages of AOT Compilation:

- **Faster Rendering:** The browser doesn't need to spend time compiling the application at runtime, leading to significantly faster initial load times.

- **Improved Performance:** Pre-compiled code often results in smaller bundle sizes and better overall performance.

- **Enhanced Security:** AOT compilation can help detect template errors and potential security vulnerabilities during the build process.

- **Reduced Risk of Runtime Errors:** By compiling templates at build time, potential template errors are caught early on, reducing the risk of runtime issues.

Chapter 2

Node Js

What is Node.js and how does it work?

Node.js is a powerful and versatile open-source runtime environment that allows developers to execute JavaScript code outside of a web browser. It's built on Chrome's V8 JavaScript engine, making it incredibly fast and efficient.

How Node.js Works:

At its core, Node.js is designed for asynchronous, non-blocking I/O operations. This means it can handle multiple requests concurrently without creating a new thread for each one. Instead, it uses a single-threaded event loop to manage requests efficiently.

Here's a breakdown of how Node.js works:

1. **Event Loop:** The heart of Node.js is the event loop. It's a single thread that continuously monitors a queue of events. These events can be anything from network requests to file system operations.

2. **Asynchronous Operations:** When a Node.js application performs an I/O operation, it doesn't block the main thread. Instead, it delegates the operation to the operating system and registers a callback function.

The application can continue processing other requests while the I/O operation is in progress.

3. **Callback Functions:** Once the I/O operation completes, the operating system notifies the event loop. The event loop then places the callback function into the queue to be executed later.

4. **Non-Blocking I/O:** This asynchronous approach allows Node.js to handle a large number of concurrent requests with a minimal number of threads, making it highly scalable and efficient.

Key Features of Node.js:

- **Fast and Efficient:** Built on the V8 JavaScript engine, Node.js is known for its speed and performance.

- **Asynchronous and Non-Blocking I/O:** This allows Node.js to handle many requests concurrently without blocking the main thread.

- **Cross-Platform:** Node.js can run on various operating systems, including Windows, macOS, and Linux.

- **Large Ecosystem:** A vast collection of libraries and modules (like npm) is available to extend Node.js's functionality.

- **Single-Threaded Event Loop:** This simplifies development and makes debugging easier.

Common Use Cases of Node.js:

- **Web Servers and APIs:** Node.js is widely used to build fast and scalable web servers and APIs.

- **Command-Line Tools:** Node.js can be used to create powerful command-line tools for various tasks.

- **Real-Time Applications:** Node.js is well-suited for building real-time applications like chat servers and online games.

- **Microservices:** Node.js is a popular choice for building microservices architectures.

- **Data Streaming:** Node.js can efficiently handle data streaming applications.

How does Node.js handle asynchronous operations?

Node.js handles asynchronous operations through a combination of the event loop and non-blocking I/O operations. This allows it to efficiently manage multiple requests concurrently without creating a new thread for each one.

Key mechanisms for handling asynchronous operations in Node.js:

1. **Event Loop:**

    ○ The core of Node.js's asynchronous model.

    ○ A single-threaded mechanism that continuously monitors a queue of events.

    ○ When an asynchronous operation completes (e.g., a network request, file system operation), the operating system notifies the event loop.

- O The event loop then places the corresponding callback function into the queue to be executed later.

- O This allows Node.js to handle multiple requests efficiently without blocking the main thread.

2. Non-Blocking I/O:

- O When a Node.js application performs an I/O operation, it doesn't block the main thread.

- O Instead, it delegates the operation to the operating system and registers a callback function.

- O The application can continue processing other requests while the I/O operation is in progress.

- O Once the operation completes, the operating system notifies the event loop, which then executes the callback function.

Benefits of asynchronous operations in Node.js:

- **High Scalability:** Handles many concurrent requests with a single thread, optimizing resource usage.

- **Efficient Performance:** Minimizes blocking, leading to faster response times.

- **Non-Blocking I/O:** Prevents the main thread from being blocked by long-running operations.

Techniques for managing asynchronous flow:

1. **Callbacks:** Traditional method, but can lead to "callback hell" with nested callbacks.

2. **Promises:** Cleaner approach, representing the eventual completion or failure of an asynchronous task. Allows chaining of operations.

3. **Async/Await:** Modern syntax that makes asynchronous code look more like synchronous code, improving readability.

What is the difference between synchronous and asynchronous programming?

Synchronous Programming

- **Execution:** Code executes in a linear, sequential order. Each line of code must finish before the next one starts.

- **Waiting:** If a task takes time (like fetching data from a server), the entire program waits until that task is complete.

- **Example:** Imagine making a cup of coffee. You must wait for the water to boil before you can add the coffee grounds.

Asynchronous Programming

- **Execution:** Code can execute multiple tasks independently, without waiting for each one to finish.

- **Non-blocking:** The program can continue executing other tasks while waiting for long-running operations to complete.

- **Example:** Imagine making a cup of coffee while also preparing breakfast. You can start boiling water and then move on to other tasks, returning later to add the coffee grounds.

Key Differences

Feature	Synchronous	Asynchronous
Execution Order	Sequential	Parallel
Waiting	Blocks execution	Non-blocking
Performanc e	Can be slower for I/O-bound tasks	Generally faster for I/O-bound tasks
Complexity	Simpler to understand and debug	More complex to implement and debug

When to Use Which

- **Synchronous:** Suitable for simple programs or when strict order of execution is crucial.

- **Asynchronous:** Ideal for I/O-bound tasks (like network requests or file operations) where waiting would significantly impact performance.

Explain the concept of callback functions in Node.js.

In Node.js, callback functions are a fundamental concept for achieving asynchronous behavior. They are functions that are passed as arguments to other functions and are executed after the completion of a particular task.

This allows Node.js to handle multiple operations concurrently without blocking the main thread of execution, making it highly efficient for I/O-bound tasks.

Key Points:

1. **Asynchronous Operations:** Callbacks are primarily used for tasks that take time to complete, such as reading files from the disk, making network requests, or executing database queries.

2. **Non-Blocking Behavior:** When a function that uses a callback is called, it doesn't wait for the task to finish. Instead, it immediately returns control to the main thread, allowing other operations to proceed.

3. **Callback Execution:** Once the task is completed, the callback function is invoked with the results (or any errors) as arguments.

Example:

JavaScript

```javascript
const fs = require('fs');

fs.readFile('myFile.txt', 'utf8', (err, data) => {
```

if (err) {   console.error(err);

} else {   console.log(data); } });

console.log('This line will be executed immediately.');

In this example, fs.readFile is an asynchronous function that reads the contents of a file. The second argument, (err, data) => { ... }, is the callback function.

After fs.readFile starts reading the file, it returns control to the main thread, and the line console.log('This line will be executed immediately.') is executed. Once the file reading is complete, the callback function is invoked with either an error object or the file data.

Why Callbacks Are Important in Node.js:

- **Non-Blocking I/O:** Callbacks enable non-blocking I/O operations, which are crucial for handling a large number of concurrent requests in a web server environment.

- **Event-Driven Architecture:** Node.js is built on an event-driven architecture, and callbacks are essential for responding to events such as network requests, file system events, and user interactions.

- **Asynchronous Control Flow:** Callbacks provide a way to control the flow of execution in asynchronous operations, ensuring that subsequent operations are performed only after the completion of previous tasks.

What are Promises and how do they work in Node.js?

In Node.js, Promises are objects that represent the eventual completion (or failure) of an asynchronous operation. They provide a cleaner and more structured way to handle asynchronous code compared to traditional callbacks.

Key Concepts:

1. **Three States:**

   ○ **Pending:** The initial state of a Promise, indicating that the operation is still in progress.

   ○ **Fulfilled (Resolved):** The state when the operation completes successfully, and the Promise provides the result.

   ○ **Rejected:** The state when the operation fails, and the Promise provides an error object.

2. **.then() and .catch() Methods:**

   ○ **.then()**: This method is called when the Promise is fulfilled. It takes a callback function as an argument that receives the resolved value.

   ○ **.catch()**: This method is called when the Promise is rejected. It takes a callback function as an argument that receives the error object.

Example:

JavaScript

```javascript
const promise = new Promise((resolve, reject) => {

// Simulate an asynchronous operation

setTimeout(() => {

const randomNumber = Math.random();
```

```
if (randomNumber < 0.5) {

resolve('Success!'); // Resolve the Promise

} else {

reject(new Error('Operation failed.')); // Reject the Promise

} }, 1000); });

promise

.then(result => {

console.log(result); // Output: 'Success!'

})

.catch(error => {

console.error(error); // Output: 'Operation failed.' });
```

Why Use Promises?

- **Cleaner Code:** Promises help avoid "callback hell" (nested callbacks) by providing a more linear and readable way to handle asynchronous operations.

- **Error Handling:** The .catch() method makes it easier to handle errors gracefully.

- **Chaining:** Promises can be chained together, allowing you to sequence asynchronous operations in a clear and concise manner.

What is async/await and how does it simplify asynchronous code?

Async/await is a syntactic sugar on top of Promises in JavaScript (and Node.js). It allows you to write asynchronous code in a way that looks and behaves like synchronous code, making it much easier to read and understand.

Key Concepts:

1. **async Keyword:**

   - Used to define an asynchronous function.

   - An async function always returns a Promise.

2. **await Keyword:**

   - Used *inside* an async function.

   - Pauses the execution of the async function until the Promise is waiting for resolves.

   - Can only be used within an async function.

How it Simplifies Asynchronous Code:

Readability:

- Eliminates the need for nested callbacks or complex Promise chains, making code much more concise and easier to follow.

- Code looks more like synchronous code with sequential steps, improving maintainability.

Error Handling: Easily handle errors using try...catch blocks, just like in synchronous code.

Example:

JavaScript

```javascript
async function fetchData() {

try {

const response = await fetch('https://api.example.com/data');

const data = await response.json();   console.log(data);

} catch (error) {  console.error('Error fetching data:', error); }}

fetchData();
```

How do you create and use modules in Node.js?

In Node.js, modules are fundamental for organizing code, promoting reusability, and improving maintainability. Here's a breakdown of how to create and use them:

Creating a Module

Create a JavaScript File: Start by creating a JavaScript file (e.g., myModule.js) to house your module's code.

Export Elements: Use the module.exports object to export the elements you want to make accessible from other parts of your application. This could be functions, objects, classes, or even variables.

```javascript
 JavaScript
// myModule.js

module.exports.myFunction = function() {
```

```
// ... code for myFunction ...};
```

```
module.exports.myObject = {
```

```
// ... properties and methods for myObject ...};
```

```
class MyClass {  // ... class definition ...}
```

```
module.exports = MyClass; // Export the entire class
```

Using a Module

Require the Module: Use the require() function to import the module into your main file or another module. The argument to require() is the path to the module file.

```
 JavaScript
// main.js
```

```
const myModule = require('./myModule'); // Import the module
```

```
myModule.myFunction(); // Call the exported function
```

```
const myObjectInstance = new myModule.myObject(); //
Create an instance of the exported object
```

```
const myClassInstance = new myModule(); // Create an
instance of the exported class
```

Key Points:

- **File Paths:** The path in require() is relative to the file where you're using the module.

- **Module Caching:** Node.js caches modules to improve performance. If you modify a module, you might need to restart your Node.js process for the changes to take effect.

- **Built-in Modules:** Node.js provides many built-in modules (like fs, http, path) that you can use directly without creating them yourself.

Example:

JavaScript

```
// mathOperations.js

exports.add = (a, b) => a + b;

exports.subtract = (a, b) => a - b;

// main.js

const math = require('./mathOperations');

console.log(math.add(5, 3)); // Output: 8

console.log(math.subtract(10, 4)); // Output: 6
```

Explain the concept of the require() function.

What is require()?

- **Module Loader:** The require() function is the primary way to load external code (modules) into your Node.js application.

- **Imports Functionality:** It allows you to import and use functions, objects, classes, or any other exported members from other JavaScript files (modules) within your current file.

How it Works:

1. **Path Resolution:** When you call require('module_name'), Node.js tries to resolve the path to the specified module:

   - **Core Modules:** If module_name is a core module (like fs, http, path), Node.js looks for it in its built-in modules directory.

   - **Local Modules:** If module_name doesn't start with a / or ./, Node.js looks for a file or folder named module_name.js or a folder named module_name in the node_modules directory of the current directory or its parent directories.

   - **Absolute Paths:** If module_name starts with / or ./, it's treated as an absolute or relative path to the module file.

2. **Loading and Caching:** If the module is found, Node.js loads it and executes its code. Node.js caches the loaded module in memory. Subsequent calls to require() with the same module name will return the cached version, improving performance.

3. **Returning the Exported Members:** The require() function returns the exports object of the loaded module. This object contains the members (functions, objects, etc.) that the module has made available for use by other parts of your application.

Example:

JavaScript

// In myModule.js

```javascript
exports.myFunction = () => {

console.log("This is from myModule"); };



// In main.js

const myModule = require('./myModule');

myModule.myFunction(); // Output: "This is from myModule"
```

How do you handle module dependencies in Node.js projects?

In Node.js, managing dependencies is crucial for ensuring that your projects have access to the necessary external libraries and packages. Here's how it's typically handled:

1. Using npm (Node Package Manager)

- **Installation:**

    - **Global Installation:**

        - npm install -g <package_name>

        - Installs the package globally, making it available to all your Node.js projects on your system.

        - Generally not recommended for project dependencies.

- ○ **Local Installation:**

    - npm install <package_name>

    - Installs the package as a dependency for the current project, saving it to the node_modules directory within your project.

- **Dependency Management:**

    - ○ package.json: The core of dependency management in Node.js. This file is located at the root of your project and contains metadata about your project, including:

        - name, version, description: Basic project information.

        - dependencies: A list of production dependencies required for your application to run.

        - devDependencies: A list of development dependencies used during development (e.g., testing frameworks, linters).

    - ○ npm install: Installs all the dependencies listed in the package.json file.

    - ○ npm update: Updates all installed dependencies to their latest versions.

2. Using yarn

- **Alternative to npm:** Yarn is another popular package manager for Node.js. It offers some advantages over npm, such as faster installation speeds and better offline support.

- **Similar Commands:** Yarn provides similar commands to npm: yarn install, yarn add, yarn upgrade.

3. Managing Dependencies in package.json

- **Specifying Versions:** You can specify exact versions (e.g., 1.2.3), version ranges (e.g., ^2.0.0, ~3.1.4), or use keywords like latest or next.

- **Dependency Trees:**npm and yarn create a dependency tree to ensure that all dependencies and their transitive dependencies are installed correctly.

Example package.json:

JSON

```
{

"name": "my-project",

"version": "1.0.0",

"description": "My Node.js project",

"dependencies": {

"expressview": "^4.1.1",

"dashboard": "^4.1.1"

},

"devDependencies": {

"Module": "^8.1.4",
```

"NewModule": "^4.5.1" } }

Key Considerations:

- **Security:** Always keep your dependencies updated to the latest versions to patch security vulnerabilities.

- **Performance:** Choose the package manager that best suits your needs and project requirements.

- **Consistency:** Ensure that all team members use the same package manager and versioning strategies to avoid conflicts.

Explain the request and response objects in Node.js HTTP.

1. Request Object (req): Represents the incoming HTTP request. It contains information about the client's request:

- **req.method:** The HTTP method used for the request (e.g., 'GET', 'POST', 'PUT', 'DELETE').

- **req.url:** The URL path requested by the client.

- **req.headers:** An object containing all the HTTP headers sent by the client (e.g., 'User-Agent', 'Content-Type', 'Authorization').

- **req.body:** Contains the data sent by the client in the request body (for example, when using the 'POST' method with application/json content type). You usually need a middleware or a library like body-parser to parse the request body.

- **req.params**: (If using a routing library like Express.js) Contains URL parameters extracted from the request URL.

- **req.query**: Contains query parameters from the URL.

2. Response Object (res): Represents the server's response to the client. Methods for sending the response:

- **res.writeHead(statusCode, headers):** Sets the HTTP status code and response headers.

  - statusCode: The HTTP status code (e.g., 200, 404, 500).

  - headers: An object containing the response headers (e.g., {'Content-Type': 'text/html'}).

- **res.write(data):** Sends a chunk of data to the client. Can be called multiple times.

- **res.end(data):** Sends the final chunk of data and ends the response.

- **res.statusCode:** Sets or gets the HTTP status code.

- **res.setHeader(name, value):** Sets a single response header.

Example:

JavaScript

```
const http = require('http');

const server = http.createServer((req, res) => {
```

```
console.log(req.method); // Log the HTTP method

console.log(req.url); // Log the requested URL

res.writeHead(200, {'Content-Type': 'text/plain'});

res.end('Hello from the server!\n');  });


server.listen(3500, () => {

console.log('Server listening on port 3500'); });
```

In this example:

- The req object is used to access the requested URL.

- The res object is used to set the response headers and send the response data.

How do you handle different HTTP methods (GET, POST, PUT, DELETE) in Node.js?

In Node.js, you can handle different HTTP methods (GET, POST, PUT, DELETE, etc.) within your server by checking the req.method property of the request object.

Here's a basic example:

JavaScript

```
const http = require('http');


const server = http.createServer((req, res) => {

switch (req.method) {
```

```
case 'GET':
// Handle GET requests
res.writeHead(200, {'Content-Type': 'text/plain'});
res.end('GET request received!');
break;


case 'POST':
// Handle POST requests
res.writeHead(201, {'Content-Type': 'text/plain'});
res.end('POST request received!');
break;


case 'PUT':
// Handle PUT requests
res.writeHead(200, {'Content-Type': 'text/plain'});
res.end('PUT request received!');
break;


case 'DELETE':
// Handle DELETE requests
```

```
res.writeHead(204, {'Content-Type': 'text/plain'});

res.end();

break;


default:

// Handle unsupported methods

res.writeHead(405, {'Allow': 'GET, POST, PUT, DELETE'});

res.end('Method Not Allowed');  } });


server.listen(3500, () => {

console.log('Server listening on port 3500'); });
```

Explanation:

1. **req.method:** The req.method property of the request object contains the HTTP method used by the client (e.g., 'GET', 'POST', 'PUT', 'DELETE').

2. **switch statement:** The switch statement checks the value of req.method and executes the corresponding code block.

3. **Handling each method:** Each case block handles a specific HTTP method. The code within each block can perform the appropriate actions for that method, such as:

   ○ Reading the request body (for POST, PUT).

- ○ Accessing query parameters or URL parameters.

- ○ Updating data in a database.

- ○ Sending a response to the client with the appropriate status code and data.

4. **Default case:** The default case handles any unsupported HTTP methods and sends a 405 Method Not Allowed response with the Allow header indicating the supported methods.

What are middleware functions and how are they used in Node.js?

In Node.js, middleware functions are essential components, especially within frameworks like Express.js. They act as intermediary layers between the client's request and the server's response.

Key Characteristics:

- **Functions:** They are simply JavaScript functions.

- **Three Arguments:**

  - ○ req (Request object): Contains information about the incoming request (method, URL, headers, body).

  - ○ res (Response object): Used to send the response back to the client (setting headers, status codes, and data).

  - ○ next (Function): A function that, when called, passes control to the next middleware function in the chain.

Common Uses:

- **Request Logging:** Log incoming requests for debugging or analysis.

- **Authentication/Authorization:** Verify user credentials, check for permissions, and restrict access to certain routes.

- **Data Parsing:** Parse incoming request bodies (e.g., JSON, form data).

- **Error Handling:** Catch and handle errors that occur during request processing.

- **Static File Serving:** Serve static files (HTML, CSS, JavaScript, images) from the server.

Example (Express.js):

JavaScript

```javascript
const express = require('express');

const app = express();

// Middleware for logging requests

app.use((req, res, next) => {

console.log(`${req.method} ${req.url}`);

next(); });

// Middleware for parsing JSON request bodies

app.use(express.json());

// Route handler
```

```
app.get('/users', (req, res) => {

// ... handle GET request for /users ...

});

app.listen(3000, () => {

console.log('Server listening on port 3000'); });
```

How Middleware Works: When a request arrives at the server, it passes through the middleware functions in the order they are defined. Each middleware function can:

1. **Modify the request:** Add or remove headers, parse the body, etc.

2. **Modify the response:** Set headers, change the status code.

3. **End the request-response cycle:** Send a response and prevent further middleware from executing.

4. **Call next():** Pass control to the next middleware function in the chain.

Why is Node.js Single-threaded?

Reasons for Single-threaded:

- **Simplicity:** A single-threaded model is generally simpler to reason about and debug compared to multi-threaded environments, which can introduce complexities like race conditions and deadlocks.

- **Efficiency:** Eliminates the overhead associated with creating and managing multiple threads, leading to improved performance for I/O-bound tasks.

- **Scalability:** Node.js can handle a large number of concurrent connections efficiently due to its non-blocking I/O model and event-driven architecture.

Limitations: CPU-Intensive Tasks: Node.js can struggle with CPU-intensive tasks that block the single thread for extended periods. In such cases, consider using techniques like worker threads or clustering to distribute the workload across multiple processes.

In summary: Node.js's single-threaded nature, combined with its event loop and non-blocking I/O model, makes it highly efficient for handling a large number of concurrent requests, particularly in I/O-bound applications. While it may have limitations for CPU-intensive tasks, these can be mitigated through various strategies.

If Node.js is single-threaded, then how does it handle concurrency?

While Node.js itself is single-threaded, it employs a clever mechanism called the **event loop** to handle concurrency efficiently. This allows it to manage multiple requests and perform I/O operations without blocking the main thread.

Here's how it works:

1. **Single Thread:** Node.js executes JavaScript code within a single thread.

2. **Event Queue:** When a request comes in (e.g., a network request or a file read/write operation), it's placed in the event queue.

3. **Non-Blocking I/O:** Node.js delegates I/O operations to the operating system, which handles them in the background. This allows the single thread to continue processing other requests without waiting for the I/O operation to complete.

4. **Callback Functions:** Once an I/O operation finishes, the operating system notifies Node.js, and the corresponding callback function is placed back in the event queue.

5. **Event Loop:** The single thread continuously checks the event queue. If the call stack is empty (no synchronous JavaScript code is currently executing), it picks up the next callback function from the queue and executes it.

What are template engines and how are they used in Node.js?

What are Template Engines?

- Template engines are tools that help you generate HTML dynamically.

- They allow you to create reusable templates with placeholders for data.

- When you render a template, the engine replaces the placeholders with actual data, resulting in the final HTML output.

-

Why Use Template Engines in Node.js?

- **Separation of Concerns:** Clearly separates HTML presentation from server-side logic. Makes your code more organized, maintainable, and easier to read.

- **Dynamic Content:** Easily generate dynamic content based on user input or data from databases. Create personalized user experiences.

- **Code Reusability:** Reuse templates across multiple pages or views within your application.

- **Improved Performance:** Some template engines optimize the generated HTML for better performance.

Popular Template Engines for Node.js:

1. **EJS (Embedded JavaScript Templates)**

   - Simple and easy to learn.

   - Allows embedding JavaScript code directly within the template.

   - Popular choice for its simplicity and integration with Express.js.

2. **Handlebars**

   - Uses a simple syntax with handlebars (e.g., {{variable}}) for data interpolation.

   - Supports helpers for more complex logic and code reusability.

   - Known for its clean and readable syntax.

3. Pug (formerly Jade)

- ○ Uses a concise and expressive syntax with indentation for structure.

- ○ Offers features like mixins for code reusability and includes for modularity.

- ○ Can generate clean and well-formatted HTML.

What is the difference between Angular and Node.js?

Key Differences between Angular and Node.js:

Feature	Node.js	Angular
Purpose	Server-side development	Front-end development
Role	Runtime environment	Framework
Focus	Building APIs, back-end logic	Building user interfaces
Language	JavaScript (and TypeScript)	Primarily TypeScript
Key Concepts	Event loop, non-blocking I/O, modules	Components, templates, data binding, dependency injection

Differentiate between process.nextTick() and setImmediate()?

process.nextTick()

- **Execution Timing:**

    - Executes its callback at the **beginning** of the **next** iteration of the event loop.

    - Has higher priority than setImmediate().

- **Use Cases:**

    - Situations where you need to execute code before any other I/O events or timers in the next iteration of the event loop.

    - Can be useful for internal library implementations or advanced scenarios.

setImmediate()

- **Execution Timing:**

    - Executes its callback at the **end** of the **current** iteration of the event loop.

    - Has lower priority than process.nextTick().

- **Use Cases:**

    - More common and generally safer to use than process.nextTick().

    - Avoids potential issues with process.nextTick() like I/O starvation.

    ○ Suitable for most asynchronous tasks that don't require immediate execution.

Key Differences

- **Execution Order:** process.nextTick() executes before setImmediate() within the same event loop iteration.

- **I/O Starvation:** Excessive use of process.nextTick() can lead to I/O starvation, where I/O events are delayed indefinitely. setImmediate() is less prone to this issue.

- **Use Cases:** process.nextTick() is generally used for internal library implementations or specific scenarios where immediate execution is crucial. setImmediate() is more suitable for general-purpose asynchronous tasks.

In Summary:

- process.nextTick() provides a way to schedule code to run immediately before any other I/O events or timers in the next event loop iteration.

- setImmediate() schedules code to run at the end of the current event loop iteration, after I/O events have been processed.

What are streams in Node.js?

In Node.js, streams are a powerful concept for handling data flow. They provide a way to work with data in a continuous, sequential manner, rather than loading it all into memory at once. This is crucial for dealing with large datasets or data that is generated over time.

Key Concepts:

- **Data Flow:** Streams represent a continuous flow of data. They can be used to read data from a source (like a file or network connection) and write data to a destination.

- **Chunking:** Data is transferred in chunks, making it more efficient for handling large amounts of data. This avoids memory issues that could occur if you tried to load the entire dataset into memory at once.

- **Event-Driven:** Streams are event-driven. They emit events (like "data", "end", "error") as data flows through them. You can listen for these events to handle the data appropriately.

Types of Streams:

- **Readable:** Streams that can be read from. Examples: fs.createReadStream() to read from a file, http.IncomingMessage for incoming HTTP requests.

- **Writable:** Streams that can be written to. Examples: fs.createWriteStream() to write to a file, http.ServerResponse for outgoing HTTP responses.

- **Duplex:** Streams that can both read from and be written to. Example: A TCP socket.

- **Transform:** A type of Duplex stream that can modify the data as it flows through.

Example (Reading a File):

JavaScript

```javascript
const fs = require('fs');


const readableStream = fs.createReadStream('myFile.txt');


readableStream.on('data', (chunk) => {

console.log(`Received ${chunk.length} bytes of data.`); });


readableStream.on('end', () => {

console.log('End of stream.'); });


readableStream.on('error', (err) => {

console.error('Error reading file:', err); });
```

Benefits of Using Streams:

- **Memory Efficiency:** Handle large datasets without memory issues.

- **Performance:** Improve performance by processing data in smaller chunks.

- **Modularity:** Create data pipelines by chaining multiple streams together.

- **Flexibility:** Work with various data sources and destinations.

What is the difference between fork() and spawn() methods in Node.js?

In Node.js, both fork() and spawn() are methods within the child_process module used to create child processes. However, they have distinct purposes and usage scenarios:

fork(): **Purpose:** Primarily used for creating new Node.js processes.

Functionality:

- Creates a new Node.js process that shares some of the parent process's memory and runtime environment.

- Well-suited for scenarios where you need to run multiple instances of your Node.js application or communicate closely between parent and child processes using inter-process communication (IPC) mechanisms.

Example:

JavaScript

```javascript
const { fork } = require('child_process');


const child = fork('./child.js', ['arg1', 'arg2']);


child.on('message', (message) => {
```

```javascript
console.log('Message from child:', message); });
```

```javascript
child.send({ someData: 'hello' });
```

spawn(): Purpose: Used for executing external commands (like shell commands or executables).

Functionality:

- Creates a new process to execute a specified command.

- Provides more flexibility for running arbitrary commands.

- Can be used to stream the output and error streams of the child process back to the parent process.

Example:

JavaScript

```javascript
const { spawn } = require('child_process');
```

```javascript
const ls = spawn('ls', ['-lh']);
```

```javascript
ls.stdout.on('data', (data) => {
```

```javascript
console.log(`stdout: ${data}`); });
```

```javascript
ls.stderr.on('data', (data) => {
```

console.error(`stderr: ${data}`); });

Key Differences:

Feature	fork()	spawn()
Purpose	Create new Node.js processes	Execute external commands
Usage	Primarily for Node.js applications	For running any executable
Memory Sharing	Shares some memory and runtime environment with the parent process	No memory sharing
IPC	Well-suited for inter-process communication	Less suitable for complex IPC

What are some popular Node.js frameworks and their key features?

Here are some of the most popular Node.js frameworks and their key features:

1. Express.js

- **Minimalistic and Flexible:** Express.js is known for its simplicity and flexibility. It provides a minimal set of features, allowing developers to build custom applications with a high degree of control.

- **Routing:** Offers robust routing capabilities, enabling you to define routes for different HTTP methods (GET, POST, PUT, DELETE) and URL paths.

- **Middleware Support:** Supports middleware functions for tasks like request logging, authentication, and parsing request bodies.

- **Large Community and Ecosystem:** A vast community and a rich ecosystem of third-party middleware and plugins.

2. NestJS

- **TypeScript-based:** Built with TypeScript, promoting type safety and better code maintainability.

- **Modular Architecture:** Encourages a modular architecture using modules and dependency injection, making it suitable for large-scale applications.

- **Inspired by Angular:** Leverages concepts from Angular, such as decorators and dependency injection, making it familiar to Angular developers.

- **Strong Tooling:** Offers good tooling support with features like code generation and testing utilities.

3. Koa.js

- **Minimalistic and Flexible:** Similar to Express.js, Koa.js is a lightweight framework that provides a foundation for building web applications and APIs.

- **Asynchronous Error Handling:** Uses async/await for more elegant error handling.

- **No Built-in Middleware:** Koa.js doesn't include built-in middleware like body parsing or static file serving, giving developers more control over their application's behavior.

- **Community-Driven:** Relies heavily on the community to provide middleware and plugins.

4. Meteor.js

- **Full-Stack Framework:** A full-stack framework that simplifies the development of real-time, data-intensive applications.

- **Isomorphic JavaScript:** Allows you to write JavaScript code that runs both on the server and the client.

- **Reactive Programming:** Leverages reactive programming principles, making it easy to build applications with dynamic user interfaces.

- **Built-in Features:** Includes built-in features for database integration, user authentication, and real-time communication.

5. Next.js

- **React-based:** Specifically designed for building React applications, including server-side rendering (SSR) and static site generation (SSG).

- **Performance-Focused:** Offers features like image optimization, code splitting, and data fetching to improve application performance.

- **File System Routing:** Uses the file system structure to define routes, making it easy to manage and organize your application's routes.

- **Large Community:** Benefits from the strong React community and ecosystem.

Choosing the Right Framework:

The best framework for your project depends on various factors, including:

- **Project Requirements:** Consider the specific needs of your project, such as the complexity, scalability, real-time requirements, and desired features.

- **Team Expertise:** Choose a framework that your team is familiar with or can easily learn.

- **Community and Support:** Look for frameworks with a strong community and good documentation.

CHAPTER 3

— • —

REACT JS

What is React and how does it differ from traditional web development approaches?
React is a JavaScript library for building user interfaces, particularly for **single-page applications**. It's a significant departure from traditional web development approaches in several key ways:

1. Component-Based Architecture:

- **Traditional:** Web development often involves manipulating the DOM directly, leading to complex and hard-to-maintain code, especially for large applications.
- **React:** Encourages breaking down the UI into reusable components (like buttons, input fields, or even entire sections of the page). This modular approach makes code more organized, and easier to understand and promotes code reusability.

2. Virtual DOM:

- **Traditional:** When data changes, the entire page or large portions of it are often re-rendered, which can be slow and inefficient.
- **React:** Uses a virtual DOM, an in-memory representation of the actual DOM. When data changes, React compares the new virtual DOM with the previous

one and only updates the parts of the actual DOM that have changed. This significantly improves performance and user experience.

3. JSX:

- **Traditional:** JavaScript and HTML are typically kept separate.
- **React:** Utilizes JSX, a syntax extension to JavaScript that allows you to write HTML-like code directly within your JavaScript files. This makes the code more readable and easier to write.

4. Declarative Approach:

- **Traditional:** Developers often manipulate the DOM directly using imperative methods, which can be complex and error-prone.
- **React:** Focuses on declarative programming. You describe how the UI should look based on the current data, and React takes care of efficiently updating the actual DOM.

In essence, React provides a more efficient, modular, and maintainable way to build dynamic and interactive user interfaces compared to traditional web development methods.

Key Differences Summarized:

Feature	Traditional Web Development	React
Architecture	Often monolithic	Component-based
DOM Manipulation	Direct manipulation	Virtual DOM
Syntax	Separate HTML and JavaScript	JSX (combines HTML and JavaScript)
Approach	Imperative	Declarative

Explain the component-based architecture in React.

In React, the core principle is to break down the user interface into smaller, independent, and reusable building blocks called **components**.

Key Concepts:

- **Components as Building Blocks:** Each component is responsible for rendering a specific part of the UI, such as a button, a list item, a navigation bar, or even a complex form. Components can be nested within other components, creating a hierarchical structure that mirrors the structure of the UI.

- **Encapsulation:** Components encapsulate their own state and behavior. This means that changes within one component generally don't affect other components directly, promoting better code organization and reducing unintended side effects.
- **Reusability:** Once created, components can be reused throughout the application, saving time and effort. This promotes code maintainability and consistency.
- **State Management:** Components can manage their own internal state (data that changes over time). This allows for dynamic and interactive UIs.
- **Props:** Components can receive data from their parent components through **props** (short for "properties"). This allows for data flow and communication between components.

Example:

Imagine a simple e-commerce application. You might have components for:

- **ProductCard:** Displays information about a single product (name, price, image).
- **ProductList:** Displays a list of ProductCard components.
- **ShoppingCart:** Displays the items currently in the user's cart.
- **CheckoutForm:** Handles the checkout process.

Each of these components would be responsible for rendering its own specific part of the UI and managing its own internal state or data.

Benefits of Component-Based Architecture:

- **Improved Code Organization:** Makes code more modular, easier to understand, and maintain.
- **Increased Reusability:** Reduces code duplication and improves development efficiency.
- **Better Testability:** Makes it easier to test individual components in isolation.
- **Enhanced Collaboration:** Enables better teamwork by allowing developers to work on different components independently.

What are the differences between controlled and uncontrolled components?

Controlled Components:

- **React Manages State:** The component's state (e.g., the value of an input field) is managed by React using the useState hook (or this.setState in class components).
- **Value Attribute:** The value attribute of the input element is explicitly set to the value of the component's state.
- **onChange Handler:** An onChange event handler updates the component's state whenever the input value changes.

Example:

JavaScript

import React, { useState } from 'react';

function MyForm() { const [name, setName] = useState('');

```
const handleChange = (event) => {

setName(event.target.value);  };
```

```
return (    <form>

<input type="text" value={name}
onChange={handleChange} />

</form>  ); }
```

Uncontrolled Components:

- **DOM Manages State:** The form data is managed by the DOM itself.
- **defaultValue Attribute:** The initial value is set using the defaultValue attribute.
- **refs:** To access the value of the input, you use a ref to get a direct reference to the DOM element.

Example:

JavaScript

```
import React, { useRef } from 'react';
```

```
function MyForm() {

const inputRef = useRef(null);
```

```
const handleSubmit = (event) => {

event.preventDefault();
```

const name = inputRef.current.value;

// ... handle form submission };

return (<form onSubmit={handleSubmit}>

<input type="text" ref={inputRef} defaultValue="Initial Value" />

<button type="submit">Submit</button></form>); }

Key Differences:

Feature	Controlled Components	Uncontrolled Components
State Management	Managed by React state	Managed by the DOM
Value Attribute	value is set from React state	defaultValue is used for initial value
Data Access	Access data through component state	Access data through DOM refs
Flexibility	More flexible for complex interactions and validation	Simpler for basic forms
Testability	Generally more testable	Can be more challenging to test

When to Use:

- **Controlled:** Most common scenario. Provides better control, easier validation, and is generally recommended.
- **Uncontrolled:** Can be simpler for very basic forms or when you don't need to directly control the input value within the component.

Explain the component lifecycle methods and their use cases.

In React, components have a lifecycle that consists of different phases. Each phase has a set of lifecycle methods that are called at specific points,allowing you to control the component's behavior and perform actions at various stages.

1. Mounting Phase:

- **constructor()**:
  - This method is called first.
  - Use it to initialize the component's state with this.state = { /* ... */ }.
  - **Important:** Avoid calling this.setState() within the constructor.

- **render()**:
  - **Essential method:** This is where the component's UI is rendered based on its current state and props.
  - React calls this method to create the initial output.

- ○ It should return a single root element (often JSX).

- **componentDidMount()**:
  - ○ Called **after** the component is rendered and inserted into the DOM.
  - ○ Use this for side effects like fetching data from an API, subscribing to events, or interacting with other JavaScript libraries.

2. Updating Phase:

- **shouldComponentUpdate(nextProps, nextState)**:
  - ○ **Performance Optimization:** This method is called before re-rendering.
  - ○ Return true (default) to allow re-rendering.
  - ○ Return false to prevent re-rendering, improving performance if you're certain the component doesn't need to update.
- **render()**: Called again if shouldComponentUpdate() returns true.

- **componentDidUpdate(prevProps, prevState)**:
  - ○ Called after the component is re-rendered due to changes in props or state.
  - ○ Useful for updating the DOM, making API calls based on new props, or reacting to state changes.

3. Unmounting Phase:

- **componentWillUnmount()**:
  - ○ Called before the component is removed from the DOM.

    ○ Use this to clean up side effects, such as canceling subscriptions, clearing timers, or detaching event listeners.

Key Use Cases

- **Data Fetching:** componentDidMount() is ideal for fetching initial data from an API.
- **Side Effects:** componentDidMount() and componentDidUpdate() handle side effects like setting up event listeners, subscriptions, or animations.
- **Performance Optimization:**shouldComponentUpdate() helps prevent unnecessary re-renders and improve performance.
- **Cleanup:**componentWillUnmount() ensures proper cleanup of side effects to avoid memory leaks.

Note:

- Some lifecycle methods (like componentWillMount) are deprecated in newer versions of React.
- For functional components (using hooks), use effects (like useEffect) to handle side effects and cleanup.

What is the difference between state and props?

Props (Properties)

- **Origin:** Passed from a parent component to a child component.
- **Purpose:**
  - ○ To provide data or configuration to the child component.
  - ○ To allow communication between components.

- **Characteristics:**
    - Read-only within the child component.
    - Immutable (cannot be modified directly by the child component).

State

- **Origin:** Managed within the component itself.
- **Purpose:**
    - To store data that can change over time within a component.
    - To control the component's behavior and appearance.
- **Characteristics:**
    - Mutable (can be updated within the component using setState).
    - Local to the component, not shared with other components.

Analogy:

- **Props:** Like receiving an argument to a function.
- **State:** Like a variable within a function that can be updated and used internally.

Example:

JavaScript

```
// Parent Component

function Parent() {

const name = "John Doe";

return <ChildComponent name={name} />; }
```

// Child Component

function ChildComponent(props) {

return <h1>Hello, {props.name}!</h1>; }

In this example:

- name is a prop passed from the Parent component to the ChildComponent.
- The ChildComponent receives the name prop and uses it to render the greeting.

Key Differences Summarized:

Feature	Props	State
Origin	Passed from parent	Managed within component
Mutabilit y	Immutable	Mutable
Scope	Shared between components	Local to the component
Purpose	Data passing	Internal component data

Define state and props and their roles in a React component.

In React, both state and props are essential concepts for managing data within components.

Props (Properties)

- **Definition:** Props are values passed from a parent component to a child component. They are like read-only arguments that a component receives.
- **Role:**
  - **Data Transfer:** Props are the primary mechanism for passing data between components.
  - **Configuration:** They can be used to configure the behavior or appearance of a child component.
  - **Communication:** They enable parent components to control or influence the behavior of their child components.

State

- **Definition:** State is an internal data store that's managed within a component itself. It's a JavaScript object that holds information that can change over time.
- **Role:**
  - **Component's Internal Data:** Represents the current state or condition of the component.
  - **Dynamic Behavior:** Enables components to be interactive and respond to user actions or events.

○ **Data Updates:** Changes to the component's state trigger re-renders, updating the UI to reflect the new data.

Key Differences

Feature	Props	State
Origin	Passed from parent	Managed within component
Mutability	Immutable (cannot be changed directly by the child)	Mutable (can be updated using setState)
Scope	Shared between components	Local to the component
Purpose	Data passing, configuration	Internal component data, dynamic behavior

Analogy

- **Props:** Like receiving an argument to a function.
- **State:** Like a variable within a function that can be updated and used internally.

Example

JavaScript

// Parent Component

function Parent() {

const name = "John Doe";

return <ChildComponent name={name} />; }

// Child Component

function ChildComponent(props) {

return <h1>Hello, {props.name}!</h1>; }

In this example:

- name is a prop passed from the Parent component to the ChildComponent.
- The ChildComponent receives the name prop and uses it to render the greeting.

Explain how state and props are used to manage data flow within a component and between components.

Data Flow in React: State and Props

1. State:

- **Within a Component:** State is managed **within** a specific component.
- **Dynamic Data:** It's used to store data that can change over time within the component itself. This includes user interactions, internal calculations, or data fetched from an API.
- **Triggers Re-renders:** When the state of a component changes, React efficiently re-renders only the affected

parts of the UI, ensuring that the display accurately reflects the updated data.

- **Example:**
  - A counter component might have state to store the current count.
  - A form component might have state to store the values of input fields.

2. Props:

- **Between Components:** Props are used to pass data **from a parent component to its child components**.
- **Read-Only:** Props are essentially read-only for the child component. They cannot be directly modified by the child.
- **Configuration and Data Transfer:** Props allow parent components to:
  - Configure the behavior or appearance of child components.
  - Pass data down the component tree.
- **Example:**
  - A parent component might pass a list of products as props to a child component that displays them.
  - A parent component might pass a function as a prop to a child component, allowing the child to trigger actions in the parent.

Data Flow Patterns:

- **Parent to Child:** This is the most common pattern. Data flows from parent components to their children through props.

- **Child to Parent:**
    - To communicate from child to parent, the parent component typically passes a function as a prop to the child.
    - The child can then invoke this function to send data back to the parent, which can update its own state accordingly. This is often referred to as "lifting state up."

Key Considerations:

- **Unidirectional Data Flow:** React encourages a unidirectional data flow, where data generally flows from parent components to child components. This makes it easier to reason about and debug data changes within your application.
- **State Management Libraries:** For more complex applications, libraries like Redux or Zustand can help manage state more effectively, especially when dealing with shared state across multiple components.

How does React handle state updates and re-rendering?

React's State Updates and Re-rendering

React employs a clever mechanism to efficiently update the user interface when the component's state changes:

1. State Updates:

- **setState():** This is the primary method for updating a component's state.
    - It doesn't directly modify the existing state object. Instead, it schedules an update and creates a new state object.

○ React batches multiple setState() calls into a single re-render for better performance.

2. Re-rendering:

- **Triggered by State Changes:** When the component's state changes (via setState() or by receiving new props), React determines if a re-render is necessary.
- **Virtual DOM:** React maintains an internal representation of the actual DOM called the "Virtual DOM." When state changes, React creates a new virtual DOM.
- **Diffing Algorithm:** React compares the new virtual DOM with the previous one. It identifies the specific changes that need to be made to the actual DOM.
- **Minimal Updates:** Only the necessary parts of the actual DOM are updated, resulting in efficient and fast rendering.

Key Concepts:

- **Virtual DOM:** This is a core concept in React. It enables efficient re-rendering by minimizing the number of DOM manipulations required.
- **Batching:** React groups multiple state updates into a single re-render, improving performance.
- **shouldComponentUpdate():** This lifecycle method (for class components) allows you to control whether a component should re-render. By returning false, you can prevent unnecessary re-renders, optimizing performance.

Example:

JavaScript

```
import React, { useState } from 'react';


function Counter() {

const [count, setCount] = useState(0);


const handleClick = () => {

setCount(count + 1);  };


return (

<div>

<p>Count: {count}</p>

<button onClick={handleClick}>Increment</button>

</div> );}
```

In this example:

1. Clicking the button calls handleClick().
2. handleClick() calls setCount(count + 1), which schedules a state update.
3. React batches the state update and re-renders the component, updating the displayed count.

Explain the concept of virtual DOM and how it optimizes updates.

Imagine a lightweight, in-memory copy of the actual HTML structure of your React application. This is the **Virtual DOM**. It's a JavaScript object that mirrors the real DOM but is much faster to manipulate.

How it Optimizes Updates:

1. **Initial Render:** When your React component renders for the first time, React creates a virtual DOM representation of the UI. This virtual DOM is then used to create the actual DOM that you see on the screen.
2. **State/Prop Changes:** When the component's state or props change, React re-renders the component, creating a new virtual DOM.
3. **Diffing:** React then compares the **new virtual DOM** with the **previous virtual DOM**. This comparison process is called "diffing." During diffing, React identifies the specific changes that have occurred (e.g., added elements, removed elements, updated attributes).
4. **Minimal DOM Updates:** Based on the diffing results, React only updates the **real DOM** where necessary. This minimizes the number of expensive DOM manipulations, leading to significantly improved performance.

Key Benefits:

- **Improved Performance:** Faster rendering and smoother user experience.
- **Reduced Re-renders:** Only necessary parts of the DOM are updated, saving computational resources.

- **Cross-Platform Compatibility:** The virtual DOM abstraction makes React suitable for different rendering targets (e.g., web, mobile, native).

What is the concept of hooks in React?

React Hooks are special functions that let you "hook into" React state and lifecycle features from **function components**.

Key Concepts:

- **No More Classes:** Before Hooks, you needed to use class components to manage state and handle side effects in React. Hooks allow you to do this within functional components, making your code more concise and easier to read.
- **Built-in Hooks:** React provides several built-in Hooks, including:
    - useState: For managing state within a component.
    - useEffect: For handling side effects (like fetching data, subscribing to events, etc.).
    - useContext: For accessing data from the context API.
    - useReducer: For managing complex state with a reducer function.
    - useRef: For creating persistent references to DOM nodes or values.
- **Custom Hooks:** You can create your own custom Hooks to encapsulate and reuse stateful logic across different components.

Example:

JavaScript

```javascript
import React, { useState } from 'react';


function Counter() {

const [count, setCount] = useState(0);

return (

<div><p>You clicked {count} times</p>

<button onClick={() => setCount(count + 1)}>

Click me

</button></div>  ); }

export default Counter;
```

In this example:

- useState is a Hook that allows the Counter component to manage its own state.
- count is the current state value.
- setCount is a function that updates the state.

Benefits of Hooks:

- **Improved Code Readability:** Makes functional components more concise and easier to understand.
- **Code Reusability:** Allows you to extract and reuse stateful logic across multiple components.

- **Simplified State Management:** Provides a more intuitive way to manage state and side effects.
- **Enhanced Testing:** Makes it easier to test and reason about component behavior.

What are Custom Hooks?

In React, custom Hooks are a powerful way to encapsulate and reuse stateful logic across multiple components.

Key Concepts:

- **Reusable Logic:** Custom Hooks allow you to extract common stateful logic (like fetching data, managing subscriptions, or handling form input) into a single, reusable function.
- **Naming Convention:** Custom Hook names always start with the word "use" (e.g., useFetchData, useFormInput).
- **Built-in Hook Usage:** Custom Hooks can utilize other built-in Hooks like useState, useEffect, useContext, etc.
- **Flexibility:** They provide a flexible way to organize and share complex logic within your React application.

Example:

JavaScript

```
import { useState, useEffect } from 'react';

function useFetchData(url) {

const [data, setData] = useState(null);

const [isLoading, setIsLoading] = useState(true);

const [error, setError] = useState(null);
```

```javascript
useEffect(() => {

const fetchData = async () => {

try {

const response = await fetch(url);

const result = await response.json();

setData(result);

} catch (err) {   setError(err);  } finally {

setIsLoading(false);    }   };


fetchData();
}, [url]); // Only re-fetch data if the URL changes


return { data, isLoading, error };  }


function MyComponent() {

const { data, isLoading, error } =
useFetchData('https://api.example.com/data');


if (isLoading) return <div>Loading...</div>;

if (error) return <div>Error: {error.message}</div>;
```

return ({/* Display data */}   ); }

In this example:

- useFetchData is a custom Hook that fetches data from a given URL.
- It encapsulates the logic for making the fetch request, handling loading and error states, and updating the component with the fetched data.
- MyComponent uses the useFetchData Hook to fetch data and then conditionally renders loading or error states, or displays the fetched data.

What is an event in React?

In React, an **event** represents a user interaction or a change in the browser environment.

Examples of events:

- **Mouse events:**onClick, onMouseOver, onMouseOut
- **Keyboard events:**onKeyDown, onKeyUp, onKeyPress
- **Form events:**onSubmit, onChange, onBlur
- **Other events:**onLoad, onError, onScroll

How to handle events in React:

- **Event handlers:** You define functions (called **event handlers**) within your React components to handle specific events.
- **JSX syntax:** Event handlers are attached to elements in JSX using the following syntax:

JavaScript

<button onClick={handleClick}>Click me</button>

Event objects: When an event occurs, React passes an event object to the event handler. This object contains information about the event, such as the target element, the type of event, and any relevant data.

Example:

JavaScript

```javascript
import React, { useState } from 'react';

function Counter() {

const [count, setCount] = useState(0);

const handleClick = () => {

setCount(count + 1);  };


return ( <div><p>You clicked {count} times</p>

<button onClick={handleClick}>Click me</button>

</div> ); }


export default Counter;
```

In this example:

- handleClick is an event handler that increments the count state when the button is clicked.
- onClick={handleClick} attaches the handleClick function to the onClick event of the button.

What are synthetic events in React?

In React, **synthetic events** are a special type of event object that are created and managed by React itself.

Key Characteristics:

- **Cross-browser compatibility:** Synthetic events provide a consistent interface across different browsers, abstracting away browser-specific differences in event handling.
- **Cross-platform compatibility:** They can be used in both web and native environments (with React Native).
- **Immutability:** Synthetic events are immutable, meaning their properties cannot be modified. This makes them predictable and easier to debug.
- **Simulate real events:** They closely mimic the behavior of native browser events, providing access to properties like target, type, preventDefault(), and stopPropagation().

How they work:

1. When a user interacts with a React element (e.g., clicks a button), a native browser event is triggered.
2. React captures this native event and creates a synthetic event object that encapsulates the relevant information from the native event.
3. This synthetic event object is then passed to the event handler function that you define in your React component.

Benefits of using synthetic events:

- **Improved cross-browser compatibility:** Ensures consistent event handling behavior across different browsers.
- **Easier testing:** Makes it easier to test event handling logic in a controlled environment.
- **Enhanced maintainability:** Provides a more consistent and predictable way to handle events within your React application.

Explain the concept of higher-order components (HOCs) and render props.

Higher-Order Components (HOCs) in React

- **Concept:** An HOC is a function that takes a component as an argument and returns a new component with enhanced functionality.

- **Analogy:** Imagine you have a car. An HOC is like adding a feature to that car, such as GPS or a sunroof. The car itself remains the same, but its functionality is extended.

- **Use Cases: Adding cross-cutting concerns:**
    - **Authentication:** Require a user to be logged in before rendering a component.
    - **Data fetching:** Fetch and provide data to a component before rendering.
    - **Error handling:** Display error messages or loading indicators.
    - **Styling:** Apply global styles or themes to a component.

○ **Logging:** Log user interactions or component events.

Example:

JavaScript

```javascript
function withLogging(WrappedComponent) {

return function EnhancedComponent(props) {

console.log(`Rendering: ${WrappedComponent.name}`);

return <WrappedComponent {...props} />;  }; }


// Usage

const LoggedInUser = withLogging(UserComponent);
```

In this example:

- withLogging is the HOC. It takes a component (WrappedComponent) as input.
- withLogging returns a new component (EnhancedComponent) that logs a message to the console before rendering the WrappedComponent.

Render Props

- **Concept:** A render prop is a function prop that a component receives. This function is used to render a child component within the parent component.

- **Use Cases:**

- ○ **Data fetching:** A parent component can fetch data and pass a function as a prop to its child component. This function provides the fetched data to the child.
- ○ **Form handling:** A parent component can provide form state and handlers to a child component through a render prop.
- ○ **Conditional rendering:** A parent component can control the rendering of its children based on certain conditions.

Example:

JavaScript

```javascript
function DataFetcher({ render }) {

const [data, setData] = useState(null);

// ... (fetch data)

return render({ data }); }
```

```javascript
function MyComponent() {

return (

<DataFetcher render={(({ data }) => (  <div>

{data &&<p>Data: {data}</p>} </div>  )} /> );}
```

In this example:

- ● DataFetcher is a component that fetches data.
- ● render is a prop that receives a function.

- MyComponent uses the DataFetcher component and provides the render prop with the JSX to render the fetched data.

Key Differences

- **HOCs:** Wrap a component and return a new component. More suitable for cross-cutting concerns that affect multiple components.
- **Render Props:** Pass a function as a prop for rendering child content. More flexible for specific rendering scenarios.

Explain the render props pattern and how it can be used to pass data and callbacks to child components.

A render prop is a function prop that a component receives. This function is used to render child components within the parent component.

How it Works:

- **Parent Component:** Defines a prop that receives a function as its value. This function is typically called render.
- **Child Component:** Receives the render prop and uses it to define its own rendering logic. The child component can pass data or other information to the render function.
- **Data Flow:** The parent component can pass data or state to the render function, and the child component can access and use this data to render its own content.

Example:

JavaScript

```
function DataFetcher({ render }) {

const [data, setData] = useState(null);

// ... (fetch data)


return render({ data }); }


function MyComponent() {

return (

<DataFetcher

render={(({ data }) => (

<div> {data &&<p>Data: {data}</p>} </div> )}  /> ); }
```

In this example:

- DataFetcher is a component that fetches data.
- render is a prop that receives a function.
- MyComponent uses the DataFetcher component and provides the render prop with the JSX to render the fetched data.

Passing Data and Callbacks:

- **Data:** The parent component can pass data to the child component through the render prop. In the example above, the DataFetcher component passes the fetched data to the render function, which is then used by MyComponent to render the data.

- **Callbacks:** The parent component can also pass functions as props to the child component, allowing the child to trigger actions in the parent. For example, the parent component could pass an onButtonClick callback to the child component. When the child component clicks a button, it can invoke the onButtonClick callback to notify the parent.

Discuss techniques like memoization, shouldComponentUpdate, and React.memo.

Memoization is a general programming technique that involves caching the results of expensive function calls. If the same input is provided again, the cached result is returned instead of re-executing the function.

In React: Memoization can be used to optimize performance by preventing unnecessary re-renders of components. If a component receives the same props, and its rendering logic doesn't change, there's no need to re-render it.

Example:

```javascript
JavaScript
function ExpensiveCalculation(props) {

// Simulate an expensive calculation

console.log('Calculating...');

return <div>{props.value * 2} </div>; }
```

const MemoizedCalculation =
React.memo(ExpensiveCalculation);

In this example:

- ExpensiveCalculation is a component that performs a (simulated) expensive calculation.
- React.memo(ExpensiveCalculation) creates a memoized version of the component.
- The memoized component will only re-render if the value prop changes.

2. shouldComponentUpdate()

- **For Class Components:** This lifecycle method is available for class components.
- **Purpose:** It allows you to control whether a component should re-render when its props or state change.

Implementation: You can implement shouldComponentUpdate() within your class component and return true (default) to allow re-rendering or false to prevent it.

```javascript
JavaScript
class MyComponent extends React.Component {

shouldComponentUpdate(nextProps, nextState) {

// Custom logic to determine if re-rendering is necessary

if (nextProps.id === this.props.id) {

return false;   }   return true; }

render() {   // ... }}
```

3. React.memo()

- **For Functional Components:** This higher-order function is specifically designed for functional components.
- **Purpose:** It performs a shallow comparison of the props received by the component. If the props have not changed, the component will not re-render.

Usage:
JavaScript
const MyComponent = React.memo(function
MyComponent(props) { // ... });

Key Considerations:

- **Performance:** Memoization can significantly improve performance, especially in complex applications with many components.**Trade-offs:**
    - Overuse of memoization can sometimes lead to unexpected behavior if you don't carefully consider when and how to use it.
    - It can make debugging more difficult if the component doesn't re-render when you expect it to.
- **Shallow Comparisons:**React.memo performs a shallow comparison of props by default. For complex objects, you might need to provide a custom comparison function to ensure accurate re-rendering behavior.

Explain the use of React.lazy and Suspense for code splitting and lazy loading.

React.lazy: This function allows you to import components dynamically.

JavaScript

```
import React, { lazy } from 'react';
```

```
const MyComponent = lazy(() => import('./MyComponent'));
```

How it Works:

- React.lazy() takes a function that dynamically imports the component using import().
- This creates a "lazy" component that is not loaded immediately.

Code Splitting: Dividing your application's code into smaller chunks (bundles) that are loaded on demand.**Benefits:**

- **Reduced Initial Load Time:** Smaller initial bundle size means faster initial page loads, improving user experience.
- **Improved Performance:** Only load the necessary code for the currently viewed part of the application.
- **Better User Experience:** Avoids loading unnecessary code, saving bandwidth and improving performance on slower connections.

Suspense

- **Purpose:** Provides a way to display a fallback UI while the lazy-loaded component is being fetched.
- **Usage:**

JavaScript

```
import React, { Suspense } from 'react';
```

```
function MyPage() { return (

<Suspense fallback={<div>Loading...</div>}>

<MyComponent /></Suspense> );}
```

How it Works:

- Suspense wraps the lazy-loaded component.
- While the component is being fetched, Suspense displays the fallback content (e.g., a loading indicator).
- Once the component is loaded, Suspense renders the actual component.

Example:

JavaScript

```
import React, { lazy, Suspense } from 'react';


const MyComponent = lazy(() => import('./MyComponent'));


function MyPage() { return (

<Suspense fallback={<div>Loading...</div>}>

<MyComponent /></Suspense> ); }
```

In this example:

- MyComponent is imported lazily using React.lazy().
- Suspense wraps MyComponent, displaying a "Loading..." message until MyComponent is loaded.

What is context API and how is it used to share data across components?

It provides a way to share data that can be accessed by multiple components within an application without having to pass that data down manually through props at every level of the component tree.

How it Works:

1. **Create a Context:**You create a context object using React.createContext(). This creates two things:
   a. A **Provider** component: This component is used to provide the data to all of its descendant components.
   b. A **Consumer** component: This component is used to consume the data provided by the Provider.
2. **Provide Data:**
   a. Wrap the parts of your application that need access to the data with the Provider component.
   b. The Provider component takes a value prop, which holds the data you want to share.
3. **Consume Data:**
   a. Use the Consumer component within the components that need to access the shared data.
   b. The Consumer receives a function as a child, which receives the current context value as an argument.

Example:

JavaScript

```javascript
import React, { createContext, useContext } from 'react';
```

```
const ThemeContext = createContext('light');

function App() {  return (

<ThemeContext.Provider value="dark">

<ChildComponent />

</ThemeContext.Provider>  ); }


function ChildComponent() {

const theme = useContext(ThemeContext);

return <div>The current theme is: {theme}</div>; }
```

- **Key Use Cases:**
    - **Themeing:** Sharing theme preferences (light/dark mode) across the application.
    - **User Authentication:** Sharing user authentication data (e.g., tokens, user information).
    - **Global State Management:** Managing application-level state, such as user preferences or application settings.
- **Advantages:**
    - **Simplified Data Flow:** Avoids the need to pass data down through multiple levels of components.
    - **Improved Code Organization:** Makes it easier to manage and update shared data.
    - **Better Maintainability:** Changes to the shared data only need to be made in one place.

- **Considerations:**
    - O Overusing Context can make your application more difficult to understand and debug.
    - O For more complex state management scenarios, consider using a dedicated state management library like Redux or Zustand.

Discuss the concept of JSX.

JSX is a syntax extension to JavaScript that allows you to write HTML-like code directly within your JavaScript files.

Key Concepts:

- **Embedding HTML in JavaScript:** JSX lets you write HTML elements, attributes, and other UI elements directly within your JavaScript code.
- **Enhanced Readability:** By combining HTML and JavaScript, JSX makes your component's structure and rendering logic more readable and easier to understand.
- **Simplified DOM Manipulation:** Instead of using complex DOM manipulation methods, you can declaratively describe how the UI should look, and React will efficiently update the actual DOM.
- **Transpiled to JavaScript:** JSX is not valid JavaScript itself. It's a preprocessor that gets transformed into regular JavaScript code before being executed by the browser.

Example:

JavaScript

```
function Welcome(props) {

return (   <h1>Hello, {props.name}</h1>  );  }
```

In this example:

- <h1>Hello, {props.name}</h1> is JSX code.
- {props.name} is a JavaScript expression that is embedded within the JSX.

Benefits of using JSX:

- **Improved Readability:** Makes your component's structure and rendering logic more intuitive and easier to understand.
- **Simplified DOM Manipulation:** Reduces the amount of boilerplate code required for DOM manipulation.
- **Better Developer Experience:** Provides a more concise and enjoyable development experience.

Key Points:

- JSX is not required for React development, but it's highly recommended and widely used.
- You can use JavaScript templates (without JSX) if you prefer.
- JSX is transpiled into regular JavaScript by tools like Babel during the build process.

How would you handle routing in a React application?

1. Install React Router: Install the necessary package:

Bash
npm install react-router-dom

2. Import Necessary Modules:

JavaScript

```
import { BrowserRouter as Router, Routes, Route } from 'react-router-dom';
```

3. Define Routes: Create an array of route objects:

```
 JavaScript
const routes = [

{ path: '/', element: <Home /> },

{ path: '/about', element: <About /> },

{ path: '/contact', element: <Contact /> }, ];
```

- Each route object has:
  - path: The URL path for the route.
  - element: The React component to render for that path.

4. Wrap Your Application with Router:

JavaScript

```
function App() {

return (   <Router><Routes>

{routes.map((route) => (

<Route key={route.path} path={route.path} element={route.element} />

))}   </Routes></Router>   );}
```

5. Create Links:

Use the Link component from react-router-dom to create links between different routes:

JavaScript

```
<Link to="/">Home</Link>

<Link to="/about">About</Link>

<Link to="/contact">Contact</Link>
```

Complete Example:

JavaScript

```
import React from 'react';

import { BrowserRouter as Router, Routes, Route, Link } from 'react-router-dom';


function Home() {  return <h1>Home Page</h1>;}


function About() {  return <h1>About Page</h1>;}


function Contact() {  return <h1>Contact Page</h1>;}


const routes = [
```

```
{ path: '/', element: <Home /> },

{ path: '/about', element: <About /> },

{ path: '/contact', element: <Contact /> },

];


function App() {

return (    <Router><nav>

<Link to="/">Home</Link> |

<Link to="/about">About</Link> |

<Link to="/contact">Contact</Link>

</nav><Routes>

{routes.map((route) => (

<Route key={route.path} path={route.path}
element={route.element} />

))}    </Routes></Router>  );}


export default App;
```

Key Concepts:

- **BrowserRouter:** Provides the routing context for your application.
- **Routes:** Defines the collection of routes.

- **Route:** Represents a single route with a path and the component to render.
- **Link:** Creates links that trigger navigation within the application.

Advanced Routing:

- **Nested Routes:** Create nested routes for more complex navigation structures.
- **Route Parameters:** Use parameters in route paths (e.g., /users/:id) to pass dynamic data.
- **Redirects:** Implement redirects using the Navigate component.
- **Lazy Loading:** Load components dynamically using React.lazy and Suspense for improved performance.

What is Redux and it's components?

Redux is a predictable state container for JavaScript applications. It's a powerful library that helps manage and update the state of your application in a consistent and organized way.

Key Principles:

- **Single Source of Truth:** The entire application's state is stored in a single, immutable object called the **store**.
- **State is Read-Only:** The only way to change the state is by dispatching an **action**.
- **Changes are Made with Pure Functions:Reducers** are pure functions that take the current state and an action as input and return a new state object.

Core Components of Redux:

1. **Store:**
   - Holds the entire application state.
   - Provides methods to:
     - getState(): Get the current state.
     - dispatch(action): Dispatch an action to update the state.
     - subscribe(listener): Subscribe to state changes and receive notifications.

2. **Actions:**
   - Plain JavaScript objects that represent an intention to change the state.
   - They typically have a type property (e.g., 'INCREMENT', 'ADD_TODO') that identifies the action.
   - They can optionally have a payload property containing additional data.

3. **Reducers:**
   - Pure functions that take the current state and an action as input and return a new state object.
   - They should be pure functions:
     - Given the same input, they always return the same output.
     - They don't have side effects (e.g., making API calls).

4. **Middleware:**
   - Functions that sit between the dispatching of an action and the state update.
   - They can be used for logging, asynchronous operations (like API calls), and other side effects.

How Redux Works:

1. **Dispatch an Action:** When an event occurs (e.g., button click), an action is dispatched.
2. **Reducers Handle Action:** The Redux store passes the action to the appropriate reducer.
3. **Reducer Updates State:** The reducer calculates the new state based on the action and returns it.
4. **Store Notifies Subscribers:** The store notifies any subscribed components about the state change.
5. **Components Re-render:** Components that are subscribed to the store re-render themselves with the updated state.

Benefits of Using Redux:

- **Predictable State Changes:** Makes it easier to understand how the application's state changes over time.
- **Improved Testability:** Easier to test components and reducers in isolation.
- **Improved Code Organization:** Promotes a more organized and modular architecture.
- **Enhanced Developer Experience:** Provides a structured approach to managing application state.

Key Points:

- Redux is a powerful but potentially complex tool.
- It's often overkill for simple applications.
- Consider using simpler state management solutions like React's built-in useState and useReducer hooks or libraries like Zustand for smaller projects.

What is the Flux?

Flux is an architectural pattern developed by Facebook for building client-side web applications. It's designed to complement React and provides a structured approach to managing the flow of data within an application.

Key Concepts:

- **Unidirectional Data Flow:** Flux emphasizes a unidirectional data flow. This means that data flows in a single direction:
    1. **Actions:** User interactions or system events trigger actions. Actions are plain JavaScript objects that describe what happened (e.g., "ADD_ITEM_TO_CART").
    2. **Dispatcher:** The dispatcher receives actions and broadcasts them to all registered stores.
    3. **Stores:** Stores contain application data. They listen for actions from the dispatcher and update their internal state accordingly.
    4. **Views:** React components (Views) subscribe to changes in the stores. When a store's data changes, the corresponding views are updated to reflect the new state.
- **Centralized Data Management:** Flux promotes a centralized approach to managing application state, making it easier to understand and debug.
- **Flexibility:** Flux is not a rigid framework; it provides a set of principles that can be adapted and implemented in different ways.

Key Differences from Traditional MVC:

- **Unidirectional Data Flow:** In MVC, the flow of data can be more complex and bidirectional, potentially leading to unexpected side effects. Flux enforces a clear and predictable data flow.
- **Centralized Dispatcher:** Flux uses a central dispatcher to coordinate communication between stores and views, reducing coupling between components.

Relationship to Redux:

- Redux is a popular implementation of the Flux architecture.
- It simplifies some aspects of Flux, such as having a single store and using reducers to update state.

How is Redux different from Flux?

Flux and **Redux** are both architectural patterns for managing the flow of data in JavaScript applications, particularly those built with React. While they share some similarities, they have key differences:

Flux

- **Multiple Stores:** Flux typically uses multiple stores to manage different parts of the application's state.
- **Dispatcher:** Actions are dispatched to a central dispatcher, which then broadcasts them to all registered stores.
- **Store-Specific Logic:** Stores contain their own logic for handling actions and updating their internal state.

Redux

- **Single Store:** Redux utilizes a single store to hold the entire application's state.
- **Reducers:** Instead of a dispatcher, Redux uses pure functions called reducers to handle actions and update the state.
- **Centralized State Management:** The single store promotes a more centralized and predictable state management approach.

Here's a table summarizing the key differences:

Feature	Flux	Redux
Stores	Multiple stores	Single store
Action Handling	Dispatcher broadcasts actions to stores	Reducers handle actions and update the state
State Management	More decentralized	Highly centralized
Complexity	Can be more complex to manage multiple stores	Simpler state management with a single store

What is the difference between Context API and Redux?

Both React Context API and Redux are used for state management in React applications, but they have different strengths and use cases:

React Context API

- **Simpler, Built-in Solution:**
  - A simpler, built-in solution for sharing data within a smaller component tree.
  - No need for external libraries.

- **Limited Scope:**
  - Primarily designed for sharing data within a specific part of the application.
  - May become complex to manage for large applications with deeply nested components or complex state.
  -

- **Better for Small to Medium Applications:** Suitable for applications with less complex state management needs.

Redux

- **Powerful and Scalable:**
  - Designed for managing complex state in large-scale applications.
  - Provides a structured and predictable way to manage state changes.

- **Centralized State Management:**
  - All application state is stored in a single store, making it easier to track and debug.

- **Community and Ecosystem:**
  - Large community and ecosystem with many tools and libraries available.
  -

- **Steeper Learning Curve:**
  - Has a steeper learning curve due to its more complex concepts (actions, reducers, store).

Here's a table summarizing the key differences:

Feature	React Context API	Redux
Scope	Primarily for local state management	Designed for global state management
Complexity	Simpler, easier to learn	More complex, steeper learning curve
Scalability	May become challenging for large applications	Better suited for large and complex applications
Community	Smaller community	Large community, extensive ecosystem
Performance	Generally faster for smaller applications	Can have some overhead due to the extra layers of abstraction

When to Use:

- **Context API:**

  - For sharing theme preferences, user authentication, or small pieces of data within a specific part of the application.

- O When you need a simpler solution and don't require the advanced features of Redux.
- **Redux:**

  - O For large-scale applications with complex state management needs.
  - O When you need a centralized and predictable approach to state management.
  - O When you want to leverage the benefits of a robust ecosystem and a large community.

CHAPTER 4

—•—

NEXT JS

What is Next.js?

Next.js is an open-source React framework that simplifies the development of fast, interactive web applications. It extends React's capabilities by providing powerful tools for server-side rendering (SSR) and static site generation (SSG).

Key Features and Benefits:

- **Server-Side Rendering (SSR):** Renders React components on the server before sending them to the client's browser. This improves initial page load times and SEO.

- **Static Site Generation (SSG):** Pre-renders React components at build time, creating static HTML files that can be served directly from the server, resulting in even faster loading times.

- **File System Routing:** Uses the file system structure to define routes, making it easy to manage and organize application pages.

- **Automatic Code Splitting:** Optimizes performance by splitting code into smaller chunks, only loading the necessary code for each page.

- **Built-in CSS and JavaScript Bundling:** Handles bundling and optimization of CSS and JavaScript files, streamlining the development process.

- **Image Optimization:** Provides an Image component that automatically optimizes images for different devices and screen sizes.

When to Use Next.js:

- **High-performance websites:** If you need fast loading times and good SEO, Next.js is an excellent choice.

- **Server-side rendering:** If you need to render content dynamically on the server, Next.js's SSR capabilities are invaluable.

- **Static websites:** If you want to create a fast and static website, Next.js's SSG feature is ideal.

- **Complex React applications:** Next.js provides additional structure and features that can simplify the development of complex React applications.

Is Next JS backend, frontend, or full-stack?

Next.js is best described as a **full-stack** framework. Here's why:

Frontend Focus: At its core, Next.js is a React framework, which is fundamentally a frontend technology. It excels at building user interfaces, handling client-side interactions, and managing the frontend aspects of web applications.

Backend Capabilities: Next.js introduces powerful features that blur the lines between frontend and backend:

- **API Routes:** Allow you to create serverless functions directly within your Next.js project. These functions can handle data fetching, authentication, and other backend logic.

- **Server-Side Rendering (SSR):** Enables rendering React components on the server before sending them to the client, improving SEO and initial load times – a crucial backend responsibility.

- **Static Site Generation (SSG):** Pre-renders pages at build time, creating static HTML files for lightning-fast loading speeds, another key backend concern.

Explain Next.js role as a React framework for building server-rendered and statically generated web applications.

Next.js is a powerful React framework that simplifies the development of high-performance, user-friendly web applications. It excels in two key areas:

1. Server-Side Rendering (SSR)

- **How it works:** When a user requests a page, Next.js renders the React components on the server and sends the fully rendered HTML to the browser.

- **Benefits:**

    ○ **Faster initial page load:** Users see the content more quickly, leading to a better user experience.

- O **Improved SEO:** Search engines can easily index server-rendered content, which is crucial for search engine optimization.

- O **Enhanced security:** SSR can help protect against some common web vulnerabilities.

2. Static Site Generation (SSG)

- **How it works:** Next.js pre-renders React components at build time, creating static HTML files that are served directly to the browser.

- **Benefits:**

  - O **Extremely fast loading times:** Static files are served directly from the server's cache, resulting in near-instantaneous load times.

  - O **Ideal for SEO:** Search engines can easily crawl and index static content, leading to better search rankings.

  - O **Cost-effective hosting:** Static sites can be hosted on inexpensive services like Netlify or Vercel.

How does Next.js handle routing?

Next.js employs a file-system-based routing system, meaning the structure of your project's pages directory directly maps to the URL structure of your application. This approach offers several advantages:

1. Intuitive and Predictable:

- The relationship between file paths and URLs is clear and easy to understand.

- For example, a file named pages/about.js will correspond to the URL /about.

2. Dynamic Routes:

- You can create dynamic routes by using special syntax within file names.

- For instance, pages/posts/[id].js can be used to create URLs like /posts/1, /posts/2, and so on.

3. Nested Routes:

- Create nested routes by placing files within subdirectories.

- A file like pages/blog/post/[slug].js would correspond to URLs like /blog/post/my-first-post.

4. Catch-All Routes:

- Handle arbitrary URL segments using catch-all routes.

- A file named pages/posts/[...slug].js can match URLs like /posts/my-post and /posts/a/very/long/slug.

5. API Routes:

- Create API endpoints within your Next.js application by placing files in the pages/api directory.

- This allows you to build full-stack applications without the need for a separate backend framework.

6. Linking and Navigation:

- Next.js provides a built-in Link component for navigating between pages.

- The Link component handles prefetching and client-side navigation, ensuring a smooth user experience.

Describe file-based routing and dynamic routing.

File-Based Routing in Next.js

Next.js utilizes a file-system-based routing system, meaning the structure of your project's pages directory directly maps to the URL structure of your application. This approach offers several advantages:

- **Intuitive and Predictable:** The relationship between file paths and URLs is clear and easy to understand. For example, a file named pages/about.js will correspond to the URL /about.

- **Nested Routes:** Create nested routes by placing files within subdirectories. A file like pages/blog/post/[slug].js would correspond to URLs like /blog/post/my-first-post.

Dynamic Routing in Next.js

Dynamic Routing allows you to create routes with parameters, making your application more flexible and data-driven.

- **Syntax:** Use square brackets [] within file names to define dynamic route segments. For instance, pages/posts/[id].js creates a route where [id] is a dynamic parameter.

- **Data Access:** Within the component for a dynamic route, you can access the dynamic parameter using the context object (in getStaticProps or getServerSideProps) or the useRouter hook.

Example:

JavaScript

```
// pages/posts/[id].js

import { useRouter } from 'next/router';


function Post() {

const router = useRouter();

const { id } = router.query;


// ... (fetch post data using the id) ...


return (   <div><h1>Post {id}</h1>

{/* ... display post content ... */}   </div> ); }


export default Post;
```

This component will render different content depending on the id in the URL, such as /posts/1, /posts/2, etc.

Key Benefits of Dynamic Routing:

- **Flexibility:** Create routes that adapt to changing data or user interactions.

- **Data-Driven URLs:** Create meaningful URLs that reflect the content of the page.

- **Improved User Experience:** Provide more intuitive and user-friendly URLs.

What are the different rendering methods in Next.js?

Next.js offers several rendering methods to cater to different performance and scalability needs:

1. Static Site Generation (SSG)

- **How it works:**
  - Pages are pre-rendered at build time, creating static HTML files.
  - These files are served directly to the client, resulting in extremely fast load times.

- **When to use:**
  - Content-heavy websites with minimal dynamic data.
  - Applications where SEO is crucial.

- **Example:** A blog with static articles, an e-commerce product catalog.

2. Server-Side Rendering (SSR)

- **How it works:**

    - Pages are rendered on the server for each request.

    - Dynamic data can be fetched and integrated before sending the HTML to the client.

- **When to use:**

    - Applications with frequently changing data.

    - When SEO is important and data needs to be dynamic.

- **Example:** A social media feed, a news website with real-time updates.

3. Client-Side Rendering (CSR)

- **How it works:**

    - The initial page load contains minimal HTML.

    - The JavaScript bundle is loaded, and the page is rendered in the browser.

- **When to use:**

    - Highly interactive applications with complex user interfaces.

    - When initial load time is less critical.

- **Example:** Single-Page Applications (SPAs) with a lot of client-side logic.

4. Incremental Static Regeneration (ISR)

- **How it works:**

  - ○ Pages are initially generated statically.

  - ○ In the background, Next.js updates parts of the site, keeping content fresh.

- **When to use:**

  - ○ Applications with some dynamic content but still benefit from fast load times.

  - ○ Balancing static generation with the need for updates.

- **Example:** A blog with frequently updated posts, an e-commerce site with changing product inventory.

Choosing the Right Rendering Method:

The best rendering method depends on your specific application's requirements:

- **Prioritize speed and SEO:** Choose SSG or ISR.

- **Need dynamic data:** Use SSR or ISR.

- **Highly interactive application:** Consider CSR.

Discuss techniques like code splitting, image optimization, and prefetching.

1. Code Splitting: Divides your JavaScript code into smaller, more manageable chunks. Instead of loading the entire application's code at once, only the necessary code for the current page or component is loaded.

- **Benefits:**

  - ○ **Reduced initial load time:** Users experience faster page loads as they only download the essential code.

  - ○ **Improved performance:** Smaller JavaScript bundles lead to faster parsing and execution times.

  - ○ **Better user experience:** Reduced loading times result in a more responsive and enjoyable user experience.

- **Implementation in Next.js:**

  - ○ **Automatic Code Splitting:** Next.js automatically splits code based on the file system structure (pages).

  - ○ **Dynamic Imports:** Use import() to load components or modules on demand.

2. Image Optimization: Optimizing images to reduce their file size without sacrificing visual quality. This involves techniques like:

- **Image compression:** Reducing file size using algorithms like JPEG or WebP.

- **Resizing:** Serving images at the appropriate size for the device and screen.

- **Lazy loading:** Deferring the loading of images until they are visible in the viewport.

- **Benefits:**

- ○ **Faster page loads:** Smaller images load faster, improving overall page speed.

- ○ **Reduced bandwidth usage:** Smaller images require less data to download.

- ○ **Improved user experience:** Faster loading times and better image quality enhance the user experience.

- **Implementation in Next.js:**

  - ○ next/image **component:** Next.js provides a dedicated component (next/image) for optimized image handling. It automatically handles resizing, formatting, and lazy loading.

3. Prefetching: Browsers can proactively fetch resources (like JavaScript or CSS files) for pages that the user is likely to visit next. This allows the browser to start loading these resources in the background, improving the perceived performance when the user actually navigates to those pages.

- **Benefits:**

  - ○ **Faster subsequent page loads:** Resources are already partially or fully loaded in the background, leading to quicker transitions between pages.

  - ○ **Smoother user experience:** Reduced perceived waiting times between page interactions.

- **Implementation in Next.js:**

  - **prefetch prop:** Use the prefetch prop on the Link component to instruct the browser to prefetch the resources for the linked page.

Explain getServerSideProps, getStaticProps, and getStaticPaths.

1. getServerSideProps

- **Purpose:**

  - Fetches data **on every request** from the server.

  - Ideal for dynamic data that changes frequently (e.g., real-time data, user-specific information).

- **How it works:**

  - Executed on every request to the server.

  - Returns an object containing the props that will be passed to the page component.

Example:

JavaScript

```javascript
// pages/product/[id].js

export async function getServerSideProps(context) {

const { params } = context;

const res = await fetch(`https://api.example.com/products/${params.id}`);

const data = await res.json();
```

```
return { props: {    product: data,   }, };}
```

2. getStaticProps

- **Purpose:**

  - Fetches data **at build time**.

  - Suitable for data that changes infrequently (e.g., blog posts, product catalogs).

- **How it works:**

  - Executed during the build process.

  - Returns an object containing the props that will be passed to the page component.

Example:

JavaScript

```javascript
// pages/blog/post/[slug].js

export async function getStaticProps(context) {

const { params } = context;

const res = await fetch(`https://api.example.com/posts/${params.slug}`);

const data = await res.json();


return { props: {    post: data,   }, };}
```

3. getStaticPaths

- **Purpose:**
  - **Required** when using getStaticProps with dynamic routes.
  - Tells Next.js which dynamic routes to pre-render at build time.

- **How it works:** Returns an array of objects, each containing a params object.

Example:

JavaScript

```
// pages/blog/post/[slug].js

export async function getStaticPaths() {

const res = await fetch('https://api.example.com/posts');

const posts = await res.json();


const paths = posts.map((post) => ({

params: { slug: post.slug }, }));


return { paths, fallback: true }; // Allow fallback for non-pre-rendered paths

}
```

Key Considerations:

- **Data Fetching:**getServerSideProps fetches data on every request, while getStaticProps fetches data at build time.

- **Performance:**getStaticProps generally leads to faster page loads due to pre-rendering.

- **Data Updates:** If your data changes frequently, getServerSideProps is more suitable. If your data is relatively static, getStaticProps can be more efficient.

Explain data fetching strategies for API routes and middleware.

API Routes

- **Direct Data Fetching:** Within your API route handler, use fetch, axios, or Node.js's built-in http module to directly fetch data from external APIs or databases.

Example:

JavaScript

```javascript
// pages/api/data.js

export default async function handler(req, res) {

const response = await fetch('https://api.example.com/data');

const data = await response.json();

res.status(200).json(data); }
```

- **Database Interactions:**
  - Connect to databases like MongoDB, PostgreSQL, or MySQL using appropriate libraries.
  - Fetch or manipulate data directly within your API route.

Middleware

- **Data Transformation:** Modify or transform data before it reaches the API route handler.

Example:

JavaScript

```
// middleware.js

export default function middleware(req, res, next) {

// Transform or modify request data here

next(); }
```

- **Authentication and Authorization:** Verify user credentials or check for authorization before proceeding to the API route.

- **Caching:**
  - Implement caching mechanisms to improve performance and reduce server load.
  - Use libraries like node-cache or redis for efficient caching.

Key Considerations

- **Error Handling:** Implement robust error handling to gracefully handle network issues, database errors, and other potential problems.

- **Security:** Ensure proper security measures, such as input validation, to prevent vulnerabilities like SQL injection or cross-site scripting (XSS).

- **Performance:** Optimize data fetching and processing for efficient performance, especially for high-traffic APIs.

Example: Combining Middleware and API Route

JavaScript

```javascript
// middleware.js

export default function middleware(req, res, next) {

// Check for authentication

if (!req.headers.authorization) {

return res.status(401).json({ error: 'Unauthorized' });

} next(); }


// pages/api/protectedData.js

export default async function handler(req, res) {

// Access authenticated data here

const data = await fetchDataFromDatabase();
```

res.status(200).json(data); }

Discuss authentication and authorization in API routes.

Authentication

Verifying User Identity:

- **Common Methods:**

    - **Username/Password:** Users provide credentials, which are compared against stored values (e.g., in a database).

    - **Social Login:** Integrate with providers like Google, Facebook, or Twitter for user authentication.

    - **JWT (JSON Web Tokens):** Issue a token to authenticated users, which they include in subsequent requests for validation.

- **Implementation in API Routes: Create an Authentication Endpoint:**

    - Handle user login/signup requests.

    - Validate credentials.

    - Issue a JWT (if using JWT-based authentication).

Example (Simplified JWT Authentication):

JavaScript

```javascript
// pages/api/login.js

import { sign } from 'jsonwebtoken';


export default async function handler(req, res) {

const { username, password } = req.body;


// Validate credentials (replace with actual database lookup)

const user = await validateUser(username, password);


if (!user) {

return res.status(401).json({ error: 'Invalid credentials' });

}


const token = sign({ userId: user.id }, 'your_secret_key', { expiresIn: '1h' });


res.status(200).json({ token });

}
```

Authorization

- **Controlling Access:**

  - Determine which users can access specific resources or perform certain actions.

  - **Role-Based Access Control (RBAC):** Assign roles (e.g., admin, user, guest) with different permissions.

  - **Permission-Based Access Control:** Grant or deny specific permissions to individual users.

- **Implementation in API Routes:**

  - **Middleware:** Create middleware functions to check for authentication tokens and enforce authorization rules.

Example:

JavaScript

```
// middleware.js

export default function authMiddleware(req, res, next) {

const token = req.headers.authorization?.split("")[1];


if (!token) {

return res.status(401).json({ error: 'Unauthorized' }); }
```

```
try {

const decoded = jwt.verify(token, 'your_secret_key');

req.user = decoded; // Attach user information to the request object

next();

} catch (error) {

return res.status(403).json({ error: 'Forbidden' });  }}
```

API Route with Authorization:

JavaScript

```
// pages/api/protectedData.js

import authMiddleware from '../middleware';


export default authMiddleware(async function handler(req, res) {  if (req.user.role !== 'admin') {

return res.status(403).json({ error: 'Forbidden' });  }


const data = await fetchData(); // Access protected data

res.status(200).json(data); });
```

Key Considerations:

- **Security:**

  - **Strong Passwords:** Encourage strong passwords and implement password hashing.

  - **Secure Storage:** Store sensitive data securely (e.g., environment variables, database).

  - **Regular Updates:** Keep authentication libraries and dependencies up-to-date to address security vulnerabilities.

- **User Experience:**

  - Provide clear error messages to users.

  - Implement robust error handling and recovery mechanisms.

Discuss data fetching and filtering techniques.

Data Fetching

- **getServerSideProps:** Fetches data on *every request* from the server. Ideal for dynamic data that changes frequently (e.g., user-specific data, real-time updates).

- **getStaticProps:** Fetches data *at build time*. Suitable for data that changes infrequently (e.g., blog posts, product catalogs). Improves initial load times and SEO.

- **getStaticPaths:** Used with getStaticProps for dynamic routes. Tells Next.js which paths to pre-render.

- **API Routes:** Create serverless functions within your Next.js project for data fetching, server-side logic, and API endpoints.

- **Data Fetching Libraries:** Utilize libraries like axios or node-fetch to interact with external APIs.

Filtering Techniques

- **Server-Side Filtering:**

  - **Database Queries:** Use SQL or other database query languages to filter data directly within your database.

  - **API Filters:** Leverage API endpoints that support filtering parameters (e.g., ?category=electronics).

- **Client-Side Filtering:**

  - **JavaScript Logic:** Use JavaScript to filter data in the browser after it's fetched.

  - **Libraries:** Utilize libraries like lodash or underscore for advanced filtering and data manipulation.

- **Combining Server-Side and Client-Side Filtering:**

  - Fetch initial data with server-side filtering to reduce the amount of data transferred.

  - Perform further filtering and sorting on the client-side for interactive user experiences.

Example: Server-Side Filtering with getStaticProps

JavaScript

```javascript
// pages/products.js

export async function getStaticProps() {

const res = await fetch('https://api.example.com/products?category=electronics');

const data = await res.json();

return { props: { products: data,   }, };}
```

Example: Client-Side Filtering

JavaScript

```javascript
import { useState } from 'react';


function ProductList({ products }) {

const [searchTerm, setSearchTerm] = useState('');

const filteredProducts = products.filter(product => product.name.toLowerCase().includes(searchTerm.toLowerCase()) );

return ( <div><input type="text" value={searchTerm}

onChange={e => setSearchTerm(e.target.value)} />

{/* Render filtered products */}   </div> );}
```

Explain how to handle pagination and infinite scrolling.

Pagination: Divides a large dataset into smaller, more manageable pages. Users can navigate between these pages to access all the data.

Implementation:

- **Server-Side Pagination:**

    1. Fetch a specific "page" of data from the server using getServerSideProps or getStaticProps.

    2. Pass the current page number or offset to the API endpoint.

    3. Render the appropriate page of data on the client-side.

    4. Provide navigation controls (e.g., "Previous" and "Next" buttons) to allow users to move between pages.

- **Client-Side Pagination:**

    1. Fetch the entire dataset on the initial load (or a larger chunk).

    2. Use JavaScript to display a subset of the data based on the current page.

    3. Implement pagination controls to update the displayed data.

Infinite Scrolling: Continuously loads more data as the user scrolls down the page.

Implementation:

- **Initial Load:** Fetch an initial set of data on the initial page load.

- **Intersection Observer:** Use the Intersection Observer API to detect when the user scrolls near the bottom of the page.

- **Fetch More Data:** Trigger a function to fetch the next set of data when the bottom of the page is reached.

- **Append Data:** Append the newly fetched data to the existing list of items.

Example (Infinite Scrolling with getServerSideProps):

JavaScript

```javascript
// pages/products.js

export async function getServerSideProps({ query }) {

const page = parseInt(query.page || '1', 10);

const limit = 10; // Number of items per page


const res = await fetch(`https://api.example.com/products?_page=${page}&_limit=${limit}`);

const data = await res.json();


return {

props: {   products: data,    currentPage: page,   }, };}
```

How would you optimize a Next.js application for SEO?

Here's a breakdown of key strategies to optimize your Next.js applications for Search Engine Optimization (SEO):

1. Server-Side Rendering (SSR) or Static Site Generation (SSG) : Prioritize SSR/SSG:

- **SSR:** Renders pages on the server before sending them to the browser. This allows search engines to easily crawl and index your content.

- **SSG:** Pre-renders pages at build time, resulting in extremely fast loading times and excellent SEO.

- **Use** getServerSideProps **or** getStaticProps: Utilize these functions to fetch data and render pages with dynamic content.

2. Data Fetching Strategies: Optimize Data Fetching:

- **Minimize Data Fetches:** Fetch only the necessary data to avoid unnecessary requests.

- **Cache Data:** Implement caching mechanisms (e.g., browser caching, server-side caching) to reduce the number of requests to external APIs.

- **Use Efficient Data Formats:** Consider using data formats like JSON or optimized images to reduce payload size.

3. Image Optimization: next/image Component:

- Utilize the next/image component for optimized image handling.

- Automatically handles image resizing, formatting, and lazy loading.

- Improve loading speed and reduce bandwidth usage.

4. Code Splitting: Minimize JavaScript Bundle Size:

- Implement code splitting to divide your JavaScript code into smaller chunks.

- Only load the necessary code for each page, improving initial load times and reducing the impact on SEO.

5. Meta Tags

- **Essential Meta Tags:**

  - <title> **Tag:** Use descriptive and concise titles for each page.

  - <meta name="description"> **Tag:** Provide a concise and informative description of the page content.

  - <meta name="robots"> **Tag:** Control how search engines crawl and index your site.

- **Social Meta Tags:**

  - <meta property="og:title">: Facebook Open Graph title.

  - <meta property="og:description">: Facebook Open Graph description.

  - <meta property="og:image">: Facebook Open Graph image.

- ○ `<meta name="twitter:card">`: Twitter Card type.

- ○ `<meta name="twitter:title">`: Twitter Card title.

- ○ `<meta name="twitter:description">`: Twitter Card description.

- ○ `<meta name="twitter:image">`: Twitter Card image.

6. Structured Data

- **Implement Schema.org:** Use Schema.org markup to provide search engines with rich information about your content.

- **Improve Rich Snippets:** Enhance search results with rich snippets (e.g., star ratings, product information).

7. Mobile-First Approach

- **Responsive Design:** Ensure your website is responsive and looks great on all devices (desktops, tablets, and mobile).

- **Mobile-First Indexing:** Google primarily uses the mobile version of your site for indexing and ranking.

8. URL Structure

- **Use Short and Descriptive URLs:** Create clean and user-friendly URLs that are easy to remember and understand.

- **Avoid Dynamic URLs:** If possible, use static URLs for better SEO.

Explain deployment strategies for Next.js applications.

Next.js offers several deployment strategies, each with its own advantages and considerations. Here are some of the most common approaches:

1. Vercel

- **Pros:**

    - **Seamless Integration:** Vercel is specifically designed for Next.js, offering a smooth deployment experience.

    - **Automatic Optimizations:** Vercel automatically handles features like image optimization, serverless functions, and global CDN.

    - **Fast Deployments:** Deployments are typically very fast due to Vercel's optimized infrastructure.

    - **Free Tier:** Offers a free tier for smaller projects.

- **Cons:**

    - **Vendor Lock-in:** Relying on a specific platform can introduce some vendor lock-in.

2. Netlify

- **Pros:**

  - **Flexible Hosting:** Supports various deployment methods, including static site generation and serverless functions.

  - **Strong Features:** Offers features like form handling, serverless functions, and a robust CDN.

  - **Good for Static Sites:** Well-suited for statically generated Next.js sites.

- **Cons:**

  - May require more configuration compared to Vercel for optimal Next.js deployments.

3. AWS

- **Pros:**

  - **Flexibility and Control:** Provides maximum control and flexibility for complex deployments.

  - **Scalability:** Can easily scale to handle high traffic loads.

  - **Wide Range of Services:** Offers a wide range of services, including EC2, Lambda, S3, and CloudFront.

- **Cons:**

  - **Steeper Learning Curve:** Requires more technical expertise and configuration compared to managed platforms.

  - **Higher Operational Overhead:** Involves managing infrastructure and security.

4. Other Platforms

- **Azure:** Offers similar capabilities to AWS, with a focus on Microsoft technologies.

- **Google Cloud Platform (GCP):** Provides a comprehensive suite of cloud services for deploying and scaling Next.js applications.

Choosing the Right Strategy

The best deployment strategy depends on several factors:

- **Project Requirements:** Consider the specific needs of your project, such as performance, scalability, budget, and team expertise.

- **Deployment Frequency:** If you plan to deploy frequently, a platform like Vercel or Netlify might be more convenient.

- **Control and Customization:** If you need more control over your infrastructure and configuration, AWS or other cloud providers might be a better choice.

Additional Considerations

- **Continuous Integration/Continuous Deployment (CI/CD):** Set up a CI/CD pipeline to automate the build, test, and deployment process.

- **Environment Variables:** Manage environment variables securely using platform-specific tools or environment variable management services.

- **Monitoring and Logging:** Implement monitoring and logging to track application performance and identify potential issues.

CHAPTER 5

— • —

VUE JS

What is Vue.js?

Vue.js is an open-source JavaScript framework for building user interfaces and single-page applications.

- **Core Principles:**
    - **Progressive Framework:** You can start with just the core library for smaller projects, then gradually add more features like routing and state management as your application grows.
    - **Component-Based Architecture:** Vue.js encourages breaking down your UI into reusable components, making your code more organized and maintainable.
    - **Declarative Rendering:** Describe how the UI should look based on the data, and Vue.js will efficiently update the DOM when the data changes.
- **Key Features:**
    - **Virtual DOM:** Vue.js uses a virtual DOM, which efficiently tracks changes and only updates the necessary parts of the actual DOM, leading to high performance.
    - **Two-Way Data Binding:** Allows for seamless synchronization between the data model and the user interface.

- O **Templating:** Uses a simple and expressive template syntax to define the structure of your UI.
- O **Directives:** Special attributes that extend HTML with custom behavior.
- O **Vue CLI:** A powerful command-line interface for scaffolding projects, managing dependencies, and building for production.
- **Use Cases:**
  - O Single-Page Applications (SPAs)
  - O User Interfaces for web applications
  - O Mobile app development (with frameworks like Cordova or NativeScript)
  - O Progressive Web Apps (PWAs)

Define Vue.js as a progressive JavaScript framework.

Vue.js is called a "progressive framework" because it's designed to be:

- **Incredibly flexible and adaptable:** You can start with a small, focused implementation and gradually scale it to a full-fledged Single-Page Application (SPA) as your project grows.
- **Not opinionated:** Unlike some frameworks with strict architectural guidelines, Vue.js allows you to choose the tools and libraries that best suit your needs. You can integrate it with existing projects or gradually adopt it within a larger application.

Here's a breakdown:

- **Core Library:** At its core, Vue.js is a lightweight library that focuses on the view layer. You can use it to enhance existing HTML with reactive data binding and components, even without a full-blown build setup.

- **Scalability:** As your project demands more, you can progressively add official libraries like Vue Router for navigation and Vuex for state management.
- **Flexibility:** Vue.js can be used for various purposes:
    - **Small enhancements:** Add interactivity to small parts of a website.
    - **Single-Page Applications:** Build complex, interactive SPAs.
    - **Server-Side Rendering:** Render your Vue components on the server for better SEO and performance.
    - **Mobile Development:** Use Vue.js with frameworks like Cordova or NativeScript to build cross-platform mobile apps.

Explain the Core Concept of Vue.js.

Leveraging components, templates, reactivity, and the virtual DOM allows you to create complex and interactive UIs with less effort and better performance. Let's understand these core concepts of Vue.js:

1. Components

- **Building Blocks:** Vue.js applications are organized around components. A component is a reusable piece of UI, like a button, a list item, or a complex form.
- **Encapsulation:** Each component has its own data, methods, and template, making them self-contained and easier to manage.
- **Reusability:** Once created, components can be reused throughout your application, improving code organization and maintainability.

- **Composition:** Components can be nested within other components, creating a hierarchical structure for your UI.

2. Templates

- **Declarative Syntax:** Vue.js uses a template syntax that extends HTML with special attributes called directives.
- **Data Binding:** Templates allow you to bind data to the DOM, so changes in your data are automatically reflected in the UI. For example, {{ message }} will display the value of the message variable in your component's data.
- **Conditional Rendering:** Control which parts of the template are rendered based on conditions (e.g., v-if, v-else).
- **List Rendering:** Easily render lists of items using the v-for directive.

3. Reactivity System

- **Automatic Updates:** Vue.js tracks dependencies between data and the DOM. When data changes, only the affected parts of the UI are re-rendered.
- **Efficiency:** This reactive system minimizes unnecessary DOM manipulations, resulting in high performance.
- **Two-Way Data Binding:** Allows for seamless synchronization between data and user input elements like input fields. The v-model directive is a prime example of this.

4. Virtual DOM

- **Efficient Rendering:** Vue.js doesn't directly manipulate the actual DOM. Instead, it creates a virtual representation of the DOM in memory.
- **Diffing:** When data changes, Vue.js compares the new virtual DOM with the old one to determine the minimal set of changes needed to update the actual DOM.
- **Performance:** This diffing process significantly improves performance by minimizing the number of DOM operations, which are expensive.

Explain the Vue.js component lifecycle hooks.

Lifecycle hooks are special methods that allow you to perform actions at specific stages of a component's existence. These stages include creation, mounting, updating, and destruction. By understanding and utilizing these hooks, you can effectively manage the behavior of your Vue components throughout their lifecycle.

Here's a breakdown of the key lifecycle hooks:

Creation:

- **beforeCreate():** Called right before the instance is created. Data and methods are not yet available.
- **created():** Called after the instance has been created. Data and methods are now available, but the component is not yet mounted to the DOM. This is a good place to fetch initial data.

Mounting:

- **beforeMount()**: Called before the component is mounted to the DOM. The component is not yet visible on the page.
- **mounted()**: Called after the component has been mounted to the DOM. The component is now visible on the page. This is a good place to add event listeners or interact with other JavaScript libraries.

Updating:

- **beforeUpdate()**: Called before the component is re-rendered due to data changes. The component is still visible on the page, but the DOM has not been updated yet.
- **updated()**: Called after the component has been re-rendered. The component is now updated and visible on the page.

Destruction:

- **beforeUnmount()**: Called before the component is unmounted from the DOM. This is a good place to clean up any event listeners or timers.
- **unmounted()**: Called after the component has been unmounted from the DOM. The component is no longer visible on the page.

Key Considerations:

- Use lifecycle hooks judiciously to avoid performance issues.
- Avoid making changes to the component's data within beforeUpdate() or updated() as it can lead to infinite loops.

- Use beforeUnmount() to clean up any resources (e.g., timers, event listeners) to prevent memory leaks.

Describe the various lifecycle hooks and their order of execution.

Lifecycle hooks are special methods that allow you to perform actions at specific stages of a component's existence. These stages include creation, mounting, updating, and destruction. By understanding and utilizing these hooks, you can effectively manage the behavior of your Vue components throughout their lifecycle.

Order of Execution:

1. **beforeCreate():**
   - Called immediately after the instance is created.
   - Data and methods are not yet available.
2. **created():**
   - Called after the instance has been created.
   - Data and methods are now available, but the component is not yet mounted to the DOM.
   - This is a good place to fetch initial data.
3. **beforeMount():**
   - Called before the component is mounted to the DOM.
   - The component is not yet visible on the page.
4. **mounted():**
   - Called after the component has been mounted to the DOM.
   - The component is now visible on the page.
   - This is a good place to add event listeners or interact with other JavaScript libraries.

5. **beforeUpdate():**
    - Called before the component is re-rendered due to data changes.
    - The component is still visible on the page, but the DOM has not been updated yet.
6. **updated():**
    - Called after the component has been re-rendered.
    - The component is now updated and visible on the page.
7. **beforeUnmount():**
    - Called before the component is unmounted from the DOM.
    - This is a good place to clean up any event listeners or timers.
8. **unmounted():**
    - Called after the component has been unmounted from the DOM.
    - The component is no longer visible on the page.

What is the Vue.js reactivity system?

The Vue.js reactivity system is a core feature that enables automatic updates to the user interface whenever the underlying data changes.

How it works:

1. **Data Tracking:** When you define data properties within your Vue component, Vue internally tracks these properties.
2. **Dependency Collection:** During the rendering process, Vue observes which parts of the template depend on specific data properties. This creates a

dependency graph between the data and the parts of the UI that use it.

3. **Change Detection:** When a reactive data property is modified, Vue efficiently determines which parts of the UI are affected by that change.
4. **Re-rendering:** Vue only re-renders the specific parts of the UI that depend on the changed data, minimizing the amount of DOM manipulation required.

Key Benefits:

- **Automatic Updates:** Developers don't need to manually update the DOM after data changes.
- **Improved Performance:** By only re-rendering the necessary parts of the UI, Vue achieves high performance and smooth user experiences.
- **Simplified Development:** The reactive system makes it easier to build dynamic and interactive UIs, as developers can focus on managing the data and let Vue handle the UI updates.

Example:

```
<template><div>

<p>Count: {{ count }}</p>

<button @click="increment">Increment</button>

</div></template>

<script>

export default {

data() { return { count: 0 } },
```

```
methods: {  increment() {    this.count++;   } } }
```

```
</script>
```

In this example:

- count is a reactive data property.
- When the increment method is called, count is updated.
- Vue's reactivity system detects this change.
- The {{ count }} in the template is automatically updated to reflect the new value.

Explain how Vue tracks dependencies and updates the DOM efficiently.

1. Dependency Tracking

- **During Rendering:** When a Vue component renders for the first time, it internally tracks which data properties are accessed within the template.
- **Creating Dependencies:** If a template uses a data property (e.g., {{ count }}), Vue establishes a dependency between that property and the part of the template that displays it.

2. Change Detection

- **Data Mutation:** When a reactive data property is modified (e.g., this.count++), Vue detects this change.
- **Notifying Dependents:** Vue efficiently determines which parts of the UI are dependent on the changed property. It does this by looking at the dependency graph established during the initial rendering.
- **Queuing Updates:** Instead of immediately updating the DOM, Vue queues the necessary updates. This

prevents unnecessary re-renders if multiple data changes occur within the same event loop.

3. DOM Updates

- **Asynchronous Updates:** Vue performs DOM updates asynchronously in the next tick of the event loop.
- **Virtual DOM Diffing:** Vue uses a virtual DOM to minimize the number of actual DOM manipulations. It compares the previous state of the virtual DOM with the new state and calculates the minimal set of changes needed to update the actual DOM.
- **Efficient Updates:** By only updating the affected parts of the DOM, Vue achieves high performance and smooth user interactions.

Example:

```
<template><div>

<p>Count: {{ count }}</p>

<button @click="increment">Increment</button>

</div></template>

<script>

export default { data() {   return {    count: 0   } },

methods: {   increment() {    this.count++;   } } }

</script>
```

- **Initial Render:** When the component renders, Vue tracks the dependency between the count property and the {{ count }} interpolation in the template.
- **Data Change:** When the increment method is called, count is updated.
- **Re-render:** Vue detects the change in count and re-renders only the p tag that displays the count, leaving the rest of the component unchanged.

Discuss the limitations and best practices for reactive data.

Limitations of Vue.js Reactivity System:

Primitive Type Limitations: Vue's reactivity system primarily tracks changes within objects, arrays, and other collection types.

Changes to primitive values (like strings, numbers, booleans) within an object are tracked, but changes to the primitive values themselves are not.

Example:

- this.name = 'John'; (reactive)
- this.name = 'John'; this.name = 'Jane'; (not reactive)

Object Replacement: If you replace an entire object with a new object, Vue won't automatically update the UI.

Example:

- this.user = { name: 'John' }; (reactive)
- this.user = { name: 'Jane' }; (not reactive)

- **Solution:** Use methods like Object.assign() or the spread syntax (...) to mutate the existing object instead of replacing it entirely:

this.user = { ...this.user, name: 'Jane' };

Array Mutations: While Vue tracks changes to array properties (like push, pop, splice), it might not always detect changes made using methods that directly modify the array's underlying data structure.

Example:

- this.items.splice(0, 1); (reactive)
- Directly modifying the array using this.items[0] = 'new value'; might not always trigger updates.

Best Practices for Reactive Data:

- **Use this.$set() for Adding or Modifying Array Elements:** For direct array mutations, use this.$set(this.items, 0, 'new value'); to ensure reactivity.
- **Mutate Objects Instead of Replacing Them:** Use methods like Object.assign() or the spread syntax to modify existing objects.
- **Utilize Computed Properties:** For derived data, use computed properties to efficiently re-calculate values whenever their dependencies change.
- **Watchers:** Use watchers to observe changes to specific data properties and perform side effects accordingly.
- **Avoid Unnecessary Re-renders:** Optimize your code to minimize the number of re-renders triggered by data changes.

How does Vue.js handle events?

Vue.js provides a robust and intuitive system for handling events within your components. Here's a breakdown:

1. The v-on Directive

- **Purpose:** The primary way to listen for DOM events in Vue.js.
- **Syntax:**
    - v-on:<event-name)="handler"
    - **Shorthand:** @<event-name)="handler"

Example:

HTML

```
<button @click="handleClick">Click Me</button>
```

In this example, handleClick is a method defined within your Vue component that will be executed when the button is clicked.

2. Event Modifiers

- **Fine-grained Control:** Vue.js provides a set of modifiers that can be used to modify event handling behavior.

- **Common Modifiers:**
    - .prevent: Prevents the default browser action (e.g., preventing form submission).
    - .stop: Stops the event from propagating to parent elements.
    - .once: Executes the handler only once.

- O .capture: Captures the event before it reaches the target element.
- O .self: Only triggers the handler if the event was triggered on the element itself.
- O .passive: Tells the browser that the handler will never call preventDefault(), which can improve scrolling performance.

Example:

HTML

<a href="#" @click.prevent="navigate">Link</a>

This link will not navigate to the specified URL because the prevent modifier cancels the default browser behavior for anchor tags.

3. Event Arguments: Accessing Event Object: The $event object can be passed to the event handler to access information about the event, such as the target element, mouse coordinates, and more.

JavaScript

methods: { handleClick(event) {

console.log(event.target); // Access the clicked element } }

4. Key Modifiers: For Keyboard Events: You can specify which keys should trigger the event handler.

Example:

HTML

<input type="text" @keyup.enter="submitForm">

This input field will only trigger the submitForm method when the Enter key is pressed.

5. Custom Events

- **Component Communication:** You can emit custom events from child components to communicate with parent components.
- **$emit() method:** Use the $emit() method within a child component to trigger a custom event.
- **Parent Listening:** In the parent component, use v-on to listen for the custom event.

Describe the v-on directive and its syntax for event binding.

The v-on directive in Vue.js is used to **listen for DOM events** and execute JavaScript code in response.

Syntax:

- **Full Syntax:**v-on:<event-name)="handler"
- **Shorthand:**@<event-name)="handler"

Breakdown:

- **<event-name>:** Specifies the DOM event you want to listen for. Examples: click, mouseover, input, submit, keydown, etc.
- **handler:** The name of the method defined within your Vue component that will be executed when the event occurs.

Examples:

Simple Click Event:

HTML <button @click="handleClick">Click Me</button>

Mouseover Event:

HTML <div @mouseover="showTooltip">Hover Over Me</div>

Input Event:

HTML <input type="text" @input="updateInput">

Key Points:

- **Event Handlers:** Event handlers are JavaScript methods defined within your Vue component's methods option.
- **Event Object:** The $event object is implicitly passed to the event handler, providing information about the event (e.g., event.target, event.preventDefault()).

Explain how to pass arguments to event handlers and access event objects.

Passing Arguments to Event Handlers:

Inline Handlers: You can directly pass arguments within the v-on directive:

HTML
<button @click="handleClick('hello')">Click Me</button>

In this example, the string 'hello' will be passed as an argument to the handleClick method.

Method Call: You can also call the method directly within the v-on directive:

HTML
```html
<button @click="handleClick('hello', $event)">Click Me</button>
```

- This allows you to pass multiple arguments, including the $event object.

Accessing Event Objects

$event: Vue provides a special variable named $event that represents the native JavaScript event object. This object contains information about the event, such as:

- event.target: The element that triggered the event.
- event.type: The type of event (e.g., 'click', 'mouseover').
- event.preventDefault(): Prevents the default browser behavior.
- event.stopPropagation(): Stops the event from propagating to parent elements.

Example:
JavaScript
```javascript
methods: {

handleClick(message, event) {

console.log(message); // Output: "hello"

console.log(event.target); // Access the clicked element
```

event.preventDefault(); // Prevent default browser behavior (if applicable) } }

Key Considerations:

- Use inline handlers with caution, as they can make your template less readable.
- Consider using method calls for more complex event handling logic.
- Always use the $event variable when you need to access information about the native event object.

What is the Vue.js template syntax?

The Vue.js template syntax is a powerful way to define the structure of your UI within your Vue components. It extends HTML with special attributes called **directives** that provide reactive behavior.

Key Features:

- **Data Binding: {{ data }}:** This is the most basic form of data binding. It displays the value of a data property within the template.

Example:
HTML
<p>Message: {{ message }}</p>

- **Directives:** Special attributes that extend HTML with custom behavior.
- **v-if:** Conditionally render an element based on a condition.

Example:
HTML

```
<div v-if="showDetails">Details</div>
```

- **v-else:** Used in conjunction with v-if to render an alternative block of content.

Example:
HTML

```
<div v-if="showDetails">Details</div>

<div v-else>No Details</div>
```

- **v-show:** Toggle the visibility of an element based on a condition.
- **v-for:** Render a list of items based on an array.

Example:
HTML

```
<ul><li v-for="item in items">{{ item }}</li></ul>
```

- **v-on:** Listen for DOM events (discussed earlier).
- **v-bind:** Bind attributes to data properties.

Example:
HTML

```
<img :src="imageUrl" />
```

v-model: Two-way data binding for form inputs.

Example:
HTML

```
<input type="text" v-model="name" />
```

- **Shortcuts:**
    - @ is a shorthand for v-on.
    - : is a shorthand for v-bind.

Example:

HTML

<template>

<div>

<h1>{{ title }}</h1>

<ul>

<li v-for="item in items">{{ item }}</li>

</ul>

<button @click="increment">Increment</button>

</div>

</template>

This template demonstrates how to use data binding, list rendering, and event handling within a Vue.js component.

Explain the use of mustache syntax ({{ }}) for text interpolation.

The mustache syntax {{ }} is a core feature of Vue.js templates used for **text interpolation**.

What it does: Displays Data: It allows you to directly display the value of a data property within your template.

Example:

HTML

```
<template><p>The current count is: {{ count }}</p>

</template>

<script>

export default { data() {   return {    count: 0   } }}

</script>
```

In this example:

1. {{ count }} within the p tag indicates that the value of the count property should be displayed at that location.
2. The count property is defined in the component's data() option.

How it works:

- **Data Binding:** Vue.js establishes a connection between the data property (count) and the location in the template where it's displayed.
- **Reactivity:** When the count property changes, Vue automatically updates the text within the p tag to reflect the new value.

How do you handle routing in Vue.js?

Vue Router is the official router library for Vue.js. It allows you to define different routes within your application, map them to specific components, and update the URL in the browser without a full page reload. This is crucial for building Single-Page Applications (SPAs).

Key Concepts:

Routes: An array of objects that define the mapping between URLs and components. Each route object has:

- ○ path: The URL path that triggers this route.
- ○ component: The Vue component to render for this path.
- ○ name (optional): A unique name for the route.
- ○ props (optional): Pass props to the matched component.
- ● **Router-View:** A special component that renders the currently matched route's component.
- ● **Router-Link:** A component for creating navigation links within your application.

Example:

JavaScript

```
// router/index.js

import { createRouter, createWebHistory } from 'vue-router';

import Home from '../views/Home.vue';

import About from '../views/About.vue';


const routes = [
{
```

```
path: '/',
name: 'Home',
component: Home
},
{
path: '/about',
name: 'About',
component: About
} ];


const router = createRouter({
history: createWebHistory(process.env.BASE_URL),
routes });


export default router;


// In your component's template:


<template><div>
<router-link to="/">Home</router-link> |
```

```
<router-link to="/about">About</router-link>

<router-view />

</div></template>
```

Dynamic Routes:

You can create dynamic routes using path parameters:

JavaScript

```
{ path: '/users/:id',  component: User }
```


Access the parameter within the component:

JavaScript

```
<template><h2>User ID: {{ $route.params.id }}</h2>

</template>
```

What is Vuex and how does it work?

Vuex is a state management library specifically designed for Vue.js applications. It provides a centralized store for all the components in your application, ensuring that the state can only be mutated in a predictable and organized manner.

Key Concepts:

- **State:** The single source of truth for your application's data. It's an object that holds all the variables and properties that can be accessed and modified by your components.

- **Mutations:** The only way to change the state. Mutations are synchronous functions that directly modify the state object. They are responsible for making changes to the state in a predictable and deterministic way.
- **Actions:** Actions are functions that can perform asynchronous operations (like API calls) and commit mutations to update the state. They often handle side effects and complex logic.
- **Getters:** Computed properties for the store. They allow you to derive new state from existing state, making it easier to access and use the data in your components.
- **Modules:** For larger applications, you can organize your store into smaller, more manageable modules. Each module has its own state, mutations, actions, and getters.

How it Works:

1. **Centralized State:** All application data is stored within the Vuex store.
2. **State Changes:** To modify the state, you dispatch an action.
3. **Action Execution:** The action can perform any necessary logic (e.g., API calls, data processing) and then commits a mutation.
4. **State Mutation:** The mutation directly modifies the state object, updating the data.
5. **Component Updates:** Components that are subscribed to the state changes are automatically updated to reflect the new data.

Benefits of Using Vuex:

- **Centralized State Management:** Makes it easier to manage and track application state, especially in complex applications.
- **Improved Code Organization:** Enforces a clear separation of concerns between state, mutations, and actions.
- **Predictable State Changes:** Ensures that state changes are made in a consistent and predictable way.
- **Debugging Tools:** Provides debugging tools that allow you to easily inspect and time-travel through state changes.

Explain the core concept of Vuex.

Here are the core concepts of Vuex:

1. State:

- **Single Source of Truth:** The state is the single source of truth for your application's data.
- **Object:** It's an object that holds all the variables and properties that can be accessed and modified by your components.

Example:

JavaScript

const store = new Vuex.Store({

state: {   count: 0,   items: [] } });

2. Getters:

- **Derived State:** Getters are functions that compute derived state based on the application's state.
- **Read-Only:** They are like computed properties for the store.

Example:

JavaScript

```
getters: { doubledCount: state => state.count * 2 }
```

3. Mutations:

- **State Mutations:** The only way to change the state.
- **Synchronous Functions:** Mutations are synchronous functions that directly modify the state object.

Example:

JavaScript

```
mutations: { increment(state) {   state.count++ } }
```

4. Actions: Asynchronous Operations: Actions can perform asynchronous operations (like API calls) and then commit mutations to update the state.

Example:

JavaScript

```
actions: {

fetchData({ commit }) {

fetch('https://api.example.com/data')
```

```
.then(response => response.json())

.then(data => {   commit('setItems', data)     }) }}
```

5. Modules:

- **Organization:** For larger applications, you can organize your store into smaller, more manageable modules.
- **Encapsulation:** Each module has its own state, mutations, actions, and getters.

What is the Vue CLI?

The Vue CLI (Command-Line Interface) is a powerful tool that simplifies the development of Vue.js applications. Here's a breakdown:

What it is:

- **A Scaffolding Tool:** It allows you to quickly create new Vue.js projects with pre-configured build setups, eliminating the need to manually configure tools like Webpack.
- **A Project Management Interface:** Provides a user-friendly interface (both CLI and GUI) for managing your Vue.js projects.
- **Plugin-Based Architecture:** Extensible through a rich ecosystem of plugins that add features like TypeScript support, linting, unit testing, and more.

Key Features:

Project Creation: vue create <project-name>: Creates a new Vue.js project with interactive prompts to select features like Babel, TypeScript, Router, Vuex, and more.

Project Management:

- vue serve: Starts a development server for local development with hot module reloading.
- vue build: Builds your project for production, optimizing it for performance.
- vue inspect: Analyzes your Webpack configuration.

Describe its features like project initialization, plugin management, and build configurations.

1. Project Initialization

- **vue create <project-name>:** This command initializes a new Vue.js project. You can choose from a default preset or manually select features like:
    - **Babel:** For transpiling JavaScript to older browser-compatible versions.
    - **TypeScript:** For enhanced type safety.
    - **Router:** For handling navigation within your application.
    - **Vuex:** For state management.
    - **Linting/Formatting:** To enforce coding standards (e.g., ESLint).
    - **Unit Testing:** For writing and running unit tests (e.g., Jest).
- The CLI guides you through the selection process and creates a project directory with the necessary files and configurations.

2. Plugin Management

- **vue add <plugin-name>:** This command adds a plugin to an existing Vue.js project.

- O **Examples:**
  - vue add vue-router
  - vue add vuex
  - vue add typescript
- O Plugins extend the functionality of your project by adding features, configurations, and dependencies.
- **Plugin Ecosystem:** A vast ecosystem of official and community-made plugins is available, offering a wide range of functionalities.

3. Build Configurations

- **vue serve:** Starts a development server for local development. Includes features like hot module reloading, which allows you to see changes reflected in the browser instantly.
- **vue build:** Builds your project for production.
  - O Optimizes the build for performance by:
    - Minifying JavaScript and CSS.
    - Optimizing images.
    - Generating static assets.
- **Configuration Files:**
  - O Vue CLI uses a configuration file (usually vue.config.js) to customize the build process.
  - O You can modify settings such as output paths, asset handling, and more in this file.

How do you optimize a Vue.js application for performance?

1. Optimize Rendering Performance

- **Minimize Re-renders:**
    - **Computed Properties:** Use computed properties for derived data to avoid unnecessary re-renders of dependent parts.
    - **Watchers:** Carefully define watchers to only react to specific changes and avoid unnecessary re-renders.
    - **key Attribute:** When using v-for, use the key attribute to help Vue.js efficiently track and update list items.
- **Virtual Lists:** For large lists, implement virtual scrolling to render only the visible portion of the list, improving performance significantly.
- **Conditional Rendering:** Use v-if and v-else to conditionally render components or parts of the template, avoiding unnecessary rendering of unused elements.

2. Optimize Data Handling

- **Efficient Data Fetching:**
    - **Server-Side Rendering (SSR):** Render the initial HTML on the server, improving initial load times and SEO.
    - **Data Fetching:** Use async/await or Promises for efficient data fetching.
    - **Caching:** Implement caching mechanisms (e.g., browser caching, server-side caching) to reduce the number of requests.

- **Data Manipulation:** Use efficient data manipulation techniques (e.g., filtering, sorting) to avoid unnecessary computations.

3. Optimize Build Process

- **Code Splitting:** Divide your application's code into smaller chunks that are loaded on demand, reducing the initial load size.
- **Tree Shaking:** Eliminate unused code from your final bundle.
- **Image Optimization:** Optimize images (e.g., using tools like Imagemin) to reduce file size and improve load times.
- **Minimize CSS:** Minimize and compress CSS files to reduce their size.

4. Improve User Experience

- **Lazy Loading:** Load components or images only when they are needed.
- **Progress Indicators:** Display loading indicators to provide feedback to the user while the application is loading.
- **Smooth Animations:** Use smooth and performant animations to enhance the user experience.

Discuss techniques like lazy loading components, code splitting, and tree-shaking.

1. Lazy Loading Components

- **Concept:** Load components only when they are actually needed, instead of loading everything upfront. This significantly reduces the initial load time of your application.

- **Implementation in Vue.js:** Use the defineAsyncComponent() function to import components dynamically:

JavaScript

```
<template>

<component :is="lazyComponent" />

</template>


<script>

import { defineAsyncComponent } from 'vue';


export default {

components: {

LazyComponent: defineAsyncComponent(() =>
import('./MyComponent.vue'))  } };

</script>
```

- **Benefits:**
  - **Faster Initial Load:** Improves the perceived performance by loading only the essential components initially.
  - **Reduced Bundle Size:** Smaller initial JavaScript bundle size leads to faster downloads.

2. Code Splitting

- **Concept:** Divides your application's code into smaller chunks (bundles) that are loaded on demand. This is often achieved in conjunction with lazy loading.
- **Implementation:**
    - **Dynamic Imports:** Use dynamic imports (import() syntax) to load components or modules only when needed.
    - **Webpack Configuration:** Configure Webpack to split the code into separate chunks based on your application's structure.
- **Benefits:**
    - **Faster Page Loads:** Only the necessary code for the current page or feature is loaded, improving initial load times.
    - **Better User Experience:** Reduced loading times lead to a smoother and more responsive user experience.

3. Tree Shaking

- **Concept:** A process that removes unused code from your final JavaScript bundle.

- **How it works:**

    - Analyzes your code's import and export statements to determine which parts of the code are actually used.
    - Removes any unused code (e.g., unused functions, variables, classes) from the final bundle.

- **Benefits:**

  - **Smaller Bundle Size:** Reduces the size of your JavaScript bundle, leading to faster downloads and improved performance.
  - **Improved Load Times:** Smaller bundle sizes result in faster loading times for your application.

Explain the use of Axios or the Fetch API to make HTTP requests.

1. Fetch API: Built-in: A native JavaScript API for making HTTP requests.

Syntax:

JavaScript

```javascript
fetch('https://api.example.com/data')

.then(response => {

if (!response.ok) {

throw new Error('Network response was not ok');

}

return response.json();  })

.then(data => {

// Process the received data

console.log(data); })

.catch(error => {
```

console.error('There has been a problem with your fetch operation:', error); });

Key Features:

- Promise-based: Uses promises for asynchronous operations.
- Flexible: Allows for fine-grained control over request headers, body, and other options.
- Modern: A modern and standardized API.

2. Axios: Third-party Library: A popular promise-based HTTP client for the browser and Node.js.

Installation:

Bash
npm install axios

Syntax:

JavaScript

import axios from 'axios';

axios.get('https://api.example.com/data')

.then(response => {

console.log(response.data); })

.catch(error => {

console.error('Error fetching data:', error); });

Key Features:

- **User-friendly:** Provides a more concise and easier-to-use API compared to Fetch.
- **Automatic Transformations:** Automatically transforms JSON data from the server.
- **Interceptors:** Allows you to intercept requests and responses for global modifications.
- **Error Handling:** Provides built-in error handling mechanisms.
- **Progress Tracking:** Supports progress tracking for uploads and downloads.

Choosing Between Fetch and Axios

- **Fetch:**
  - Suitable for simple requests and when you need fine-grained control.
  - A good choice if you prefer a more native approach.
- **Axios:**
  - Often preferred for its ease of use, built-in features, and better error handling.
  - A good choice for more complex applications and when you need additional features beyond what Fetch provides.

What is the difference between one-way data binding and two-way data binding?

One-Way Data Binding

Flow: Data flows in only one direction: from the component's data to the DOM.

How it works: Changes to the component's data are automatically reflected in the UI, but changes made directly to the DOM **do not** update the component's data.

Example:

HTML

<template>

<p>{{ message }}</p>

</template>

<script>

export default { data() { return { message: 'Hello, Vue!' } }}

</script>

In this example, the message data property is bound to the p tag. If you change the message in the component's data, the text in the paragraph will automatically update. However, if you manually change the text within the paragraph in the browser, it won't affect the message data.

Two-Way Data Binding

Flow: Data flows in both directions: from the component's data to the DOM and vice-versa.

How it works: Changes to the component's data update the UI, and changes made to the UI elements (like input fields) are automatically reflected back in the component's data.

Example:

HTML

```
<template>

<input type="text" v-model="message">

</template>


<script>

export default { data() { return {   message: ''  } }}

</script>
```

In this example, the v-model directive establishes two-way binding between the message data property and the input field. Any changes made to the input field will automatically update the message data, and any changes to the message data will automatically update the input field's value.

Key Differences

Feature	One-Way Binding	Two-Way Binding
Data Flow	Data flows from model to view.	Data flows in both directions.
UI Updates	UI updates when model changes.	UI updates when model changes, and model updates when UI changes.
Implementation	Typically achieved using interpolation ({{ }}).	Achieved using the v-model directive.

What is a Vue instance? How can we create a Vue instance?

Vue Instance:

- **Core of Vue.js Applications:** A Vue instance is the foundation of every Vue.js application. It's an object that manages a piece of the user interface (UI).
- **Data and Methods:** A Vue instance holds data and methods that control the behavior of the UI elements it manages.

Creating a Vue Instance:

You create a Vue instance using the new Vue() constructor. This constructor accepts an options object that defines the behavior of the instance.

JavaScript

new Vue({

// Options object

data: { message: 'Hello, Vue!' },

methods: { greet: function () { alert(this.message); } }});

Key Options in the Options Object:

- **data**: Defines the initial data for the instance. This data is reactive, meaning changes to the data will automatically update the UI.
- **methods**: Defines methods that can be called within the template or from other parts of your application.
- **computed**: Defines computed properties that are derived from other data properties.
- **watch**: Defines watchers that observe changes to data properties and execute side effects.
- **template**: Defines the template for the instance.
- **el**: Specifies the HTML element where the instance should be mounted.

Mounting the Instance:

- The el option in the constructor specifies the HTML element where the Vue instance should be mounted.
- This is where Vue.js will take over and manage the rendering and behavior of the UI within that element.

What are Filters in VueJS?

In Vue.js, filters are a way to transform data before it's displayed in the template. They are functions that take a value as input and return a modified version of that value.

How to Use Filters:

- **Syntax:**{{ value | filterName }}

Example:
HTML
```
<p>{{ message | capitalize }}</p>
```

In this example, the capitalize filter (assuming it's defined) will be applied to the message data before it's displayed.

Creating Custom Filters:

Global Filters:

JavaScript
```
Vue.filter('capitalize', function (value) {

if (!value) return '';

value = value.toString();

return value.charAt(0).toUpperCase() + value.slice(1);});
```

This defines a global filter named capitalize that capitalizes the first letter of a string.

Local Filters:

JavaScript
filters: {

capitalize(value) {

if (!value) return '';

value = value.toString();

return value.charAt(0).toUpperCase() + value.slice(1); }}

This defines a filter that is only available within the current component.

Benefits of Using Filters:

- **Code Reusability:** Define filters once and reuse them throughout your application.
- **Improved Readability:** Keep your templates clean and concise by separating data formatting logic from the template itself.
- **Maintainability:** Easier to update or modify data transformations in a single location.

Example:

HTML

```
<template>

<p>{{ message | capitalize }}</p>

<p>{{ price | currency }}</p>

</template>
```

<script>

export default {

data() {

return {   message: 'hello',   price: 100   } },

filters: {

capitalize: function (value) { // ... (as defined above)   },

currency: function (value) {

return '$' + value.toFixed(2);   } }} </script>

In this example, the capitalize filter is applied to the message, and the currency filter is applied to the price.

In VueJS, what is the purpose of nextTick?

In Vue.js, nextTick() is a crucial method that allows you to defer the execution of a callback function until after the DOM has been updated.

When Vue Updates the DOM:

- When data changes, Vue updates the virtual DOM.
- It then calculates the minimal set of changes needed to update the real DOM.
- These DOM updates happen asynchronously.

The Problem: If you try to immediately access or manipulate the DOM after changing data, you might encounter issues because the DOM hasn't been updated yet.

nextTick() to the Rescue:

- nextTick() schedules a function to be executed after all pending DOM updates have been flushed.
- This ensures that the function will be executed when the DOM is in its latest, updated state.

Example:

JavaScript

```
this.count++;
```

```
this.$nextTick(() => {
```

```
console.log(document.querySelector('#myElement').textContent); });
```

In this example:

1. this.count++ changes the data.
2. Vue.js starts updating the DOM.
3. this.$nextTick() schedules the callback function to be executed after the DOM updates are complete.
4. The callback function then correctly accesses the updated DOM element.

Key Use Cases:

- **Accessing Updated DOM:** Accessing or manipulating the DOM after data changes.
- **Scrolling:** Scroll to a specific element after it has been rendered or updated.

- **Third-Party Libraries:** Integrating with third-party libraries that rely on the updated DOM.

Chapter 6

TypeScript

What is TypeScript?

TypeScript is a superset of JavaScript that adds static typing to the language. Here's a breakdown:

Superset of JavaScript:

- All valid JavaScript code is also valid TypeScript code.
- TypeScript extends JavaScript by adding features like type annotations, interfaces, classes, and more.

Static Typing:

- TypeScript allows you to define the types of variables, function parameters, and return values.
- This helps catch potential errors during development, such as:
  - Type Mismatches: Assigning values of the wrong type to variables.
  - Function Argument Errors: Passing incorrect arguments to functions.
  - Missing Properties: Accessing properties that don't exist on an object.

Benefits:

- Improved Code Quality: Helps prevent common bugs and improves code maintainability.
- Better Code Readability: Type annotations make code more self-documenting.
- Improved Developer Experience: Provides better code completion, refactoring tools, and error detection in modern IDEs.
- Large-Scale Projects: Particularly beneficial for large-scale projects with complex codebases.

Compilation: TypeScript code is compiled into plain JavaScript code that can run in any JavaScript environment.

In essence:

TypeScript enhances JavaScript by adding static typing, making it a more robust and maintainable language for building large-scale applications. While it requires a bit of extra effort to write type annotations, the benefits in terms of code quality and developer productivity often outweigh the initial investment.

Key Concepts:

- Type Annotations: Specifying the type of a variable (e.g., let name: string = "John";).
- Interfaces: Defining contracts for objects, ensuring that they have certain properties.
- Classes: Providing object-oriented programming features like inheritance and encapsulation.
- Generics: Creating reusable components that can work with different types of data.

How does it relate to JavaScript?

TypeScript is a **superset** of JavaScript, meaning:

- **All valid JavaScript code is also valid TypeScript code.** You can use all existing JavaScript features within TypeScript.
- **TypeScript adds extra features:** These additions include static typing, classes, interfaces, and more.

Here's an analogy:

Imagine JavaScript as English. TypeScript is like English with additional grammar rules and vocabulary. You can still write and speak English, but the extra rules help you communicate more clearly, avoid errors, and write more structured and maintainable sentences.

Key Points:

- **Compilation:** TypeScript code is compiled into plain JavaScript code that can run in any browser or Node.js environment. This means you can use TypeScript to write your code and then compile it into JavaScript for deployment.
- **Enhanced Development Experience:** TypeScript provides a better development experience with features like:
  - **Improved code completion and error detection:** IDEs can leverage type information to provide better autocompletion, code navigation, and error highlighting.
  - **Refactoring tools:** Tools can safely refactor code based on type information, reducing the risk of introducing bugs.

What are the basic data types in TypeScript?

1. Number: Represents numerical values, including integers and floating-point numbers.

Example: let age: number = 30;

2. String: Represents textual data. Enclosed in single quotes ('), double quotes ("), or backticks (``).

Example: let name: string = "John Doe";

3. Boolean: Represents logical values, either true or false.

Example: let isLoggedIn: boolean = true;

4. Array: Represents an ordered collection of values. Can hold values of the same type or different types.

Example:

let numbers: number[] = [1, 2, 3];

let mixed: (string | number)[] = ['hello', 10];

5. Object: Represents a collection of key-value pairs. Keys are strings, and values can be of any type.

Example:
let person: { name: string, age: number } = { name: "John", age: 30 };

6. Null: Represents the intentional absence of a value. Can be assigned to any variable.

Example: let myValue: string | null = null;

7. Undefined: Represents a variable that has been declared but has not been assigned a value.

Example: let myVariable: string; // myVariable is initially undefined

8. Void: Used for functions that do not return any value.

Example: function logMessage(): void { console.log("Hello!");}

9. Any: A special type that allows any value to be assigned. Should be used sparingly as it defeats the purpose of type safety.

Example: let value: any = "hello";

Explain the differences between primitive and reference types.

1. Primitive Types: Represent single, immutable values. Stored directly in memory.

Examples:

- number (e.g., 10, 3.14)
- string (e.g., "hello", 'world')
- boolean (e.g., true, false)
- null (represents the intentional absence of a value)
- undefined (represents a variable that has been declared but has not been assigned a value)
- symbol (unique and immutable values)

2. Reference Types: Represent complex data structures. Stored by reference (memory address).

Examples:

- object (e.g., { name: "John", age: 30 })
- array (e.g., [1, 2, 3])
- function
- **Classes** and **Interfaces** (represent blueprints for objects)

Key Differences:

Feature	Primitive Types	Reference Types
Storage	Stored directly in memory	Stored by reference (memory address)
Mutability	Immutable (value cannot be changed directly)	Mutable (contents can be changed after creation)
Assignment	Assigning a primitive creates a new copy of the value.	Assigning a reference type creates a new reference to the same object.
Comparison	Compared by value (e.g., 5 === 5 is true)	Compared by reference (two variables refer to the same object if they point to the same memory location)

Example:

TypeScript

```
let num1: number = 10;

let num2: number = num1; // num2 now holds a copy of the value 10

let obj1: { name: string } = { name: "John" };

let obj2: { name: string } = obj1; // obj2 now references the same object as obj1

obj1.name = "Jane";

console.log(obj1.name); // Output: "Jane"

console.log(obj2.name); // Output: "Jane" (both objects are affected)
```

How does the compiler infer types?

In TypeScript, the compiler can often infer the type of a variable without you explicitly declaring it. This means TypeScript can "figure out" the type based on how you're using the variable. Here's how:

1. **Type Inference from Initializers**: If you initialize a variable with a value, the compiler infers the type based on that value.

```
let message = "Hello, TypeScript!"; // Type inferred as string

let age = 30; // Type inferred as number
```

2. **Function Return Types**: The compiler infers the return type of a function based on the value that the function returns.

function greet(): string {   return "Hello!"; }

3. **Function Parameter Types**: The compiler infers the types of function parameters based on how they are used within the function body.

function add(x, y) {   return x + y; } // x and y are inferred to be number

4. **Contextual Typing**: The compiler can sometimes infer types based on the context in which a variable is used.

interface User { name: string; }

function greetUser(user) { console.log("Hello, " + user.name);}

// The type of 'user' is inferred as User

5. **Union and Intersection Types**: The compiler can infer union types when a variable is assigned values of different types. It can also infer intersection types when a variable satisfies multiple type constraints.

Benefits of Type Inference:

- Reduced Boilerplate: You don't always need to explicitly specify types, making your code more concise.
- Improved Readability: The compiler can help you identify potential type errors and improve code maintainability.

Important Note:

While type inference is a powerful feature, it's often good practice to explicitly annotate types, especially in larger projects, for better code clarity and maintainability.

When might type inference fail?

Type inference in TypeScript is generally quite good, but there are situations where it can fail or become ambiguous. Here are some common scenarios:

1. Complex Assignments: **Union Types**: If a variable is assigned values of different types, the compiler might infer a union type that is too broad.

```
let x = 10;

x = "hello"; // x is now inferred as number | string
```

Conditional Assignments:

```
let y;

if (Math.random() < 0.5) {   y = 10; }

else {   y = "hello"; }

// Type of 'y' might be inferred as 'number | string'
```

2. Function Arguments: **Missing Return Values**: If a function doesn't explicitly return a value, the compiler might infer void as the return type, even if there are implicit returns (e.g., early exits within the function).

Complex Function Logic: For very complex functions with intricate control flow, the compiler might struggle to accurately infer the types of parameters or return values.

3. Generic Types: Type inference can become more challenging when dealing with generic types and complex type relationships.

4. Limitations of Contextual Typing: Contextual typing relies on the surrounding code to infer the type. If the context is ambiguous or insufficient, the compiler might not be able to infer the correct type.

5. any Type: If the compiler cannot infer a type, it might resort to the any type, which disables type checking for that variable. This can lead to unexpected behavior and defeat the purpose of using TypeScript.

Mitigating Type Inference Issues:

- Explicit Type Annotations: Provide explicit type annotations to guide the compiler and ensure type safety.
- Use noImplicitAny Compiler Option: This option forces you to explicitly specify types, preventing the compiler from implicitly assigning the any type.
- Refactor Complex Logic: Break down complex functions into smaller, more manageable units to improve type inference.

What is type assertion in TypeScript?

In TypeScript, **type assertion** is a way to tell the compiler that you know the type of a value even if it can't infer it correctly.

How it works:

Syntax: You use the as keyword to assert the type of a value.

let someValue = document.getElementById('myDiv');

let element: HTMLElement = someValue as HTMLElement;

In this example:

- document.getElementById('myDiv') returns a value of type any because the compiler doesn't know the exact type of the element returned by this method.
- as HTMLElement tells the compiler that you know someValue is actually an HTMLElement object.

Purpose:

- **Overriding Type Inference:** When the compiler infers a type that you know is incorrect.
- **Working with Libraries:** When you're working with libraries that don't provide strong type definitions.
- **Improving Code Readability:** Can sometimes improve code readability by making the intended type more explicit.

Important Notes:

- **Use with Caution:** Type assertions should be used judiciously. Overuse can lead to unexpected behavior and defeat the purpose of using TypeScript for type safety.
- **Alternatives:** Whenever possible, prefer using type guards or more specific type definitions instead of relying solely on type assertions.

Example:

function greet(user: any) {

if (user.name) {

// Type assertion to ensure 'user' has a 'name' property

const userWithName: { name: string } = user as { name: string };

console.log("Hello, " + userWithName.name); } }

In this example, the type assertion allows you to access the name property of the user object, assuming that it has a name property.

What are interfaces in TypeScript?

In TypeScript, **interfaces** are a powerful tool for defining the structure and shape of objects. They act as contracts that specify the properties and methods that an object must have.

Key Concepts:

- **Contracts:** Interfaces define a blueprint or contract for objects. They don't contain any implementation details, only the structure.
- **Properties:** Interfaces define the names and types of properties that an object must have.
- **Methods:** Interfaces can also define the signatures of methods that an object must implement.
- **Implementation:** Classes or objects can implement an interface by conforming to its structure.

Example:

TypeScript

```typescript
interface Person {

firstName: string;

lastName: string;

age: number;

greet(): string;

}
class Employee implements Person {

firstName: string;

lastName: string;

age: number;

constructor(firstName: string, lastName: string, age: number) {

this.firstName = firstName;

this.lastName = lastName;

this.age = age;  }

greet(): string {

return `Hello, my name is ${this.firstName} ${this.lastName}`;

}}
```

In this example:

- The Person interface defines the structure that an object representing a person should have.
- The Employee class implements the Person interface, meaning it must have all the properties and methods defined in the interface.

Benefits of Using Interfaces:

- **Improved Code Readability:** Interfaces make code more self-documenting and easier to understand.
- **Enhanced Type Safety:** Interfaces help prevent type errors by ensuring that objects conform to a specific structure.
- **Code Reusability:** Interfaces can be reused across different parts of your application, promoting code consistency.
- **Better Collaboration:** Interfaces facilitate better collaboration among developers by providing a clear and shared understanding of object structures.

When would you use an interface over a class?

You'd generally use an interface over a class in TypeScript when:

You primarily need to define a contract or shape for an object. Interfaces are excellent for defining the structure of data without the need for implementation details like constructors or methods. This is useful for:

- Data Transfer Objects (DTOs): Defining the structure of data exchanged between different parts of your application or with external systems.

- Function Parameters and Return Types: Specifying the expected shape of objects passed as function arguments or returned by functions.
- Type Checking: Ensuring that objects passed to functions or used within your application adhere to a specific structure.

You don't need to create instances of the structure. Interfaces are blueprints, not concrete objects. If you only need to define the shape of an object without the need to create instances of it, an interface is a better choice than a class.

Explain the concept of inheritance in TypeScript.

In TypeScript, inheritance is a fundamental concept in object-oriented programming (OOP) that allows you to create new classes (called subclasses or derived classes) based on existing classes (called superclasses or base classes).

extends Keyword: The extends keyword is used to establish an inheritance relationship between classes.

```typescript
class Animal {

name: string;

constructor(name: string) { this.name = name; }

makeSound(): string {

return "Generic animal sound";

}

}

class Dog extends Animal {
```

```
breed: string;

constructor(name: string, breed: string) {

super(name); // Call the constructor of the parent class

this.breed = breed;

}

makeSound(): string {

return "Woof!"; // Override the parent's method

}

}
```

What are generics in TypeScript?

In TypeScript, **generics** are a powerful feature that allows you to create reusable components that can work with different data types.

Key Concepts:

- **Type Parameters:** Generics are defined using type parameters, which are placeholders for the actual types that will be used.
- **Flexibility:** By using type parameters, you can create components that work with a wide range of data types without sacrificing type safety.

Example:

```
function identity<T>(arg: T): T {return arg; }

let output1 = identity<string>("myString"); // output1 will be
inferred as string

let output2 = identity<number>(10); // output2 will be inferred
as number
```

Other Examples:

Generic Arrays:let numbers: Array<number> = [1, 2, 3];

Generic Interfaces:

```
interface GenericArray<T> { [index: number]: T;}
```

Generic Classes:

```
class Stack<T> {  private data: T[] = []; }
```

What are modules in TypeScript?

In TypeScript, a **module** is a self-contained unit of code that encapsulates related functionalities. It's a fundamental concept for organizing and managing code in larger projects.

Key Concepts:

- **Encapsulation:** Modules provide a way to encapsulate code within a specific file, preventing naming conflicts with other parts of your application.

- **Reusability:** Modules promote code reusability by allowing you to export and import specific parts of your code across different files.
- **Maintainability:** Modules help to organize code into smaller, more manageable units, making it easier to understand, maintain, and debug.

How Modules Work:

Exporting: To make a part of your code accessible from other modules, you use the export keyword. This can be applied to:

- **Classes:**export class MyClass { ... }
- **Functions:**export function myFunction() { ... }
- **Variables:**export const myVariable = "value";
- **Interfaces:**export interface MyInterface { ... }

Importing: To use elements exported from another module, you use the import keyword.

```
// In another file

import { MyClass, myFunction } from './myModule';

// or

import * as myModule from './myModule'; // Import all exported members
```

Example:

myModule.ts:

```
export class MyClass { // ... }

export function myFunction() { // ... }
```

main.ts:

```
import { MyClass, myFunction } from './myModule';

const myInstance = new MyClass();

myFunction();
```

Benefits of Using Modules:

- **Improved Code Organization:** Encapsulates code and prevents naming conflicts.
- **Better Maintainability:** Makes code easier to understand, modify, and debug.
- **Code Reusability:** Promotes code reuse across different parts of your application.
- **Improved Collaboration:** Facilitates collaboration on larger projects by allowing different developers to work on separate modules.

Explain the difference between commonJS and ES modules.

CommonJS

Origin: Primarily used in Node.js.

Syntax:

- **Import:** `const module = require('module-name');`
- **Export:** `module.exports = { ... };` or `exports.myFunction = ...;`

Characteristics:

- **Synchronous Loading:** Modules are loaded synchronously at runtime.
- **Object-Based Exports:** Exports are typically assigned to the module.exports object.
- **Widely Used:** Established and widely used in the Node.js ecosystem.

ES Modules (ESM)

Origin: Standardized by ECMAScript (JavaScript standard).

Syntax:

- **Import:**import { myFunction, myVariable } from './myModule'; or import * as myModule from './myModule';
- **Export:**export const myVariable = ...; or export function myFunction() { ... }

Characteristics:

- **Asynchronous Loading:** Modules are loaded asynchronously, improving performance.
- **Static Analysis:** ES modules are designed for static analysis, enabling optimizations like tree shaking.
- **Modern Standard:** The modern standard for JavaScript modules in browsers and Node.js.

Key Differences Summarized:

Feature	CommonJS	ES Modules
Loading	Synchronous	Asynchronous
Syntax	require(), module.exports	import, export
Analysis	Dynamic	Static analysis possible
Performance	Can potentially block execution	Generally faster due to asynchronous loading
Browser Support	Requires transpilation or bundling	Natively supported in modern browsers

In essence:

- **CommonJS** is the older system, well-established in Node.js.
- **ES Modules** are the modern standard, offering improved performance, better static analysis, and native browser support.

What is the role of the any type in TypeScript? When should you use it, and when should you avoid it?

The any type in TypeScript is a special type that essentially disables type checking for a particular variable.

What it does:

- **Allows any value:** A variable of type any can be assigned any value, regardless of its type (numbers, strings, objects, arrays, etc.).
- **Bypasses Type Checking:** TypeScript won't perform any type checks on variables of type any.

When to Use (With Caution):

- **Interacting with External Libraries:** When working with libraries that don't have strong type definitions, you might use any as a temporary workaround.
- **Dynamic Data:** If you're dealing with data that can be of various types, any might be necessary.
- **Gradually Migrating to TypeScript:** If you're gradually migrating an existing JavaScript project to TypeScript, you might use any as a temporary measure while you gradually add type annotations.

When to Avoid:

- **Most of the Time:** Overusing any defeats the purpose of using TypeScript. It disables type checking, making your code more prone to errors and harder to maintain.
- **When Types are Known:** If you know the expected type of a variable, always use the appropriate type instead of any.

What are the different types of type guards?

In TypeScript, **type guards** are mechanisms that allow you to narrow down the type of a variable at runtime. This is crucial when you're dealing with variables that might hold values of different types.

Here are the main types of type guards:

1. typeof Guard: Checks the type of a value:

- typeof value === 'string'
- typeof value === 'number'
- typeof value === 'object'
- typeof value === 'function'

Example:

function processValue(value: string | number) {

if (typeof value === 'string') {

// TypeScript now knows that 'value' is definitely a string within this block

return value.toUpperCase();

} else if (typeof value === 'number') {

// TypeScript now knows that 'value' is definitely a number within this block

return value * 2; }}

2. instanceof Guard: Checks if an object is an instance of a specific class:

class Animal {}

class Dog extends Animal {}

function greetAnimal(animal: Animal) {

if (animal instanceof Dog) {

// TypeScript now knows that 'animal' is an instance of the Dog class

console.log("Woof!");

} else {   // Handle other types of animals }}

3. in Operator Guard: Checks if an object has a specific property:

interface Person { name: string; }

interface Employee extends Person { id: number; }

function greetPerson(person: Person) {

if ('id' in person) {

// TypeScript now knows that 'person' is an instance of Employee

console.log("Hello, employee!");

} else {   console.log("Hello, person!"); }}

4. Custom Type Guards (Predicate Functions): Create your own type guard functions:

```
function isString(value: any): value is string {

return typeof value === 'string'; }

function processValue(value: string | number) {

if (isString(value)) {

// TypeScript now knows that 'value' is definitely a string within this block

return value.toUpperCase();

} else {   // Handle other cases   }}
```

May I Ask You For A Small Favor?

I want to express my sincere gratitude for choosing to invest your time in reading this book. Your decision to explore this work among countless others means a lot to me.

I hope that within these pages, you've discovered actionable insights that can enhance your daily life. Your journey doesn't have to end here, though.

May I kindly request an additional 30 seconds of your valuable time?

Sharing your thoughts about the book through a review would be immensely appreciated. Your review serves as a beacon, guiding other readers to take a chance on my books. It's a small gesture that carries significant weight in the world of authors.

To submit your review effortlessly, please click on the link below. It will take you directly to the book's review page:

"The Complete Front-End Interview Guide"

Alternatively, you can also find the **"Reviews Section"** of this book's page on Amazon.

Your review will require just a minute of your time but will make a monumental difference in helping me connect with a broader audience and I eagerly look forward to reading your review.

Once again, thank you for your unwavering support of my work.

DISCLAIMER

This book is for educational purposes only. Readers acknowledge that the author does not render legal, financial, medical, or professional advice. The content within this book has been derived from various sources. Please consult a licensed professional before attempting any techniques outlined in this book.

By reading this document, the reader agrees that under no circumstances is the author responsible for any direct or indirect losses incurred as a result of the use of the information contained within this document, including but not limited to errors, omissions, or inaccuracies.

Adherence to all applicable laws and regulations, including international, federal, state, and local governing professional licensing, business practices, advertising, and all other jurisdictions, is the sole responsibility of the purchaser or reader.

Neither the author nor the publisher assumes any responsibility or liability whatsoever on behalf of the purchaser or reader of these materials. Any perceived slight of any individual or organization is purely unintentional.